Brazilian Literature

By *ERICO VERISSIMO*

BRAZILIAN LITERATURE

CROSSROADS

THE REST IS SILENCE

ERICO VERISSIMO

BRAZILIAN LITERATURE

AN OUTLINE

GREENWOOD PRESS, PUBLISHERS
NEW YORK

To

S. GRISWOLD MORLEY

Foreword

THIS is a very sketchy history of Brazilian literature, and undoubtedly a defective one. My main objective in writing it was to give the American reader an idea of the march of literature in my country, from the day it was discovered up to the present year. Doubtless I have omitted the names of many authors, a sin for which I most humbly apologize to the persons involved. In writing about the last twenty years of Brazilian literary life I had no reference book of any kind to provide me with information. I had to rely on my memory, and memory, you know, is a very hazardous territory full of hidden unexpected traps. At any rate, I am sure that, in books like this one, trends and general aspects are much more important than mere author names.

I must make one more point clear. These pages were originally written to be read as a series of public lectures I delivered in January and February, 1944, at the University of California, Berkeley, and as I did not wish the audience to fall asleep, rocked by the singsong of my voice, while I was repeating monotonously authors' names and book titles in a language strange to them, once in a while I told them a story or anecdote out of some novel, short story, or poem of Brazilian literature. So, many of the passages I quote in this book were not chosen because they are the most representative of their authors or times, but only because they make good yarns or pleasant reading. The reader will certainly understand my point better if I tell him that I am not a critic, but a storyteller.

This is *not* an unbiased view of Brazilian literature. In

writing this book I did not take the position of God; I contented myself with that of a simple reader who some-times may be wrong, but who is never willing to betray his own tastes and distastes.

E. V.

San Francisco, California, 1944

Contents

Brazilian Literature

I

"So Good Is the Land . . ."

IN A small town of Brazil I saw many years ago a play staged and performed by amateurs, one of the scenes of which I will never forget. (The time was A.D. 1200, and the place somewhere in Europe.) The hero stepped over the proscenium and, beating his pasteboard cuirass with his clenched fists, cried out: "We are the brave and noble knights of the Middle Ages!"

Later on, a friend of mine told me about another melodramatic play in which the central character, a fair and gallant lad, bidding farewell to his lovely bride, recited: "Oh, my beloved one, now I am going to take part in that tremendous campaign known in history by the name of the Thirty Years' War!"

I don't believe that things could be easier or more cheerful for us, the characters in the human comedy, if we were told beforehand exactly what part we are playing and what words and deeds the Author chose for us to say and do. However, I am sure it would be much more convenient for historians if they could say or write, for instance, that the Middle Ages or the Renaissance started on August 14, at four o'clock P.M., in such or such year. Unfortunately for the essayists and fortunately for the novelists, the facts of life, as the vagaries of soul, refuse to be rigidly filed and labeled. That is why, in writing or talking about historical events, we must use frequently, if not all the time, the expression "more or less."

Let me tell you frankly that this outline of Brazilian literature has a "more or less" nature. Literature, you know, is not a science. It is a matter of taste and opinion. Brazil is also a "more or less" country, and by this I mean that we are not endowed with the scientific mind; we do not love mathematical precision. We hate numbers and formulas, but we are crazy about words, colors, and images. We are a rather Bohemian people who rely too much on God. As a matter of fact, we do really believe that God was born a Brazilian.

During almost four hundred years the intellectual life of my country kept a mirrorlike quality: it reflected the literary and artistic fashions of Europe, first through Portugal and afterward directly from Paris. But after the first two decades of the twentieth century we started a literary life of our own—of course not totally free from alien influence, because no literature is completely independent, but at least a literature concerned with Brazilian social and moral problems and speaking a Brazilian language.

I know this is no time for playing with words. Maybe I am mimicking the hero of the amateur play when I say we are living a tragic moment in history. What I am trying to say is this: "If I am now writing about such a thing as Brazilian literature it is not because I think it is really a vital subject, or that the writers and thinkers of my country are unusually important." Heavens no! I am giving you this sketchy history of Brazilian literature because I am sure that the best key to the soul of a country is the works of its writers, and I know how important it is for us North and South Americans to know each other. We need to avoid formulas. They are silly and dangerous. We Brazilians must not sum up the United States as a country of Babbitts, gangsters, greedy businessmen, and wailing crooners. And you Americans must not go on thinking that Brazil is just a land of lazy Indians, poisonous snakes, and lush palm trees. Let us try for a change to have a glimpse of the soul of both peoples. To begin with, let us examine here, no matter how briefly, the stuff Brazilians are made of. We were not asked to choose our own ancestors, nor the climate or shape of our native environment. You Americans are not *obliged* to love foreign peoples, nor are we Brazilians. But we, the inhabitants of this earth, are all in the same boat on a very uncertain and stormy voyage, and the least we can wisely do is to try to understand our traveling companions. To be understanding is to be tolerant, and tolerance is the basis of friendship and peace. And peace and friendship are our greatest concern in these troubled years.

Toward the end of the first half of the fifteenth century Europe was on a kind of honeymoon with progress. Gutenberg had invented the press. As a consequence of the capture of Constantinople by the Turks the Byzantine sages fled to Europe, bringing with them their classic treasures of culture for the Western civilization. Renaissance had dawned over the European countries, and philosophy, literature, and the arts flourished everywhere. The printed book started its promising career as a marvelous carrier of culture, knowledge, and peace, as well as a sower of unrest, rebellion, and doubt.

However, the shadowy clouds of the Middle Ages still hung over a small country at the end of the Iberian Peninsula. Not until the fourteenth century had Portugal started her life as a politically organized nation. During more than two hundred years her history was made of crude and bloody wars on the African shores, in Asia, and in the "unknown ocean." At the beginning of the sixteenth century Portugal was a powerful country of seagoing conquistadors. While Europe was divided with religious wars, the Portu-

guese, competing with the Spaniards, were trying to conquer
the rest of the world and to secure the domination of the
sea routes, as important for them as the air routes will be
after this war for the big powers of the present-day world.
Vasco da Gama discovered the sea route to the Indies, the
magic land where silk, brocades, gold, pearls, and precious
stones came from. It is said that the Casa da India, the House
of India, in Lisbon, was so rich and prosperous in those days
that sometimes it could not pay the merchants, because there
was so much money that the busy clerks had no time to
count it. Meanwhile Portugal had opened the gates of her
university to the sages of the world. It was a golden age for
the Portuguese. They were wealthy; they were glorious;
they had an empire. Art and literature were fostered, and
prospered. At the end of the sixteenth century Camões
wrote "Os Lusiadas," the famous epic poem which cele-
brates with beautiful rhythm and rhymes the feats of the
Portuguese people. The Portuguese language, derived from
the Spanish Latin, had long ago separated from the Galician
and was by now leading a life of its own.

To speak somewhat facetiously, I venture to say that
Brazil was discovered because the good old rich gentlemen
of Portugal were badly in need of hot spices to season their
food. The problem was to find a short cut to India, the land
of spices. On the threshold of the sixteenth century the King
of Portugal sent a fleet to that fabulous country; but, having
been led astray by their own fantasy, by treacherous sea
currents, or by some mischievous god, the Portuguese discovered, much to their surprise, a land that was not on their
maps, which, by the way, were the most perfect ones of the
time. The admiral decided to send some of his men ashore.
They were met by the natives, a bunch of copper-colored
fellows with high cheekbones, slanting eyes, and impene-

trable faces, who received without much fuss the many-colored beads those funny white fellows with long whiskers and queer clothes gave them as a token of friendship. Those sad-faced Indians led a very primitive life. They knew no metals and their tools and weapons were made of polished stone or wood, their condition being more or less like that of prehistoric men.

The Portuguese planted a big wooden cross near the place where they had landed, celebrated Mass, and the notary of the fleet sent a letter to his king describing the wonders and natural beauties of the land and the peculiarities of its inhabitants. After that the fleet left the unknown land, India bound, and the whole crew, from the cook to the admiral, was convinced that it was just an unimportant little island. About one year later Amerigo Vespucci, an adventurer full of daring and imagination, explored the coast of Brazil and found out it was not an island, but a very big country—a true continent. All the same, Portugal was not moved by the news. Yes, it might be a big country; but it had no gold, silver, or spices. Why waste time with such a white elephant? India was the real stuff; Brazil, just a dream. It had nice trees and colorful birds. But what was the use of trading for parrots and exotic plants when you could earn plenty of money buying precious stones, gold, and pearls in India, to exchange them in England for manufactured goods?

However, during the following years some foreign pirates disembarked on the Brazilian shores and, willing to hold on to the new land, gold or no gold, Portugal decided to colonize it, sending to its northern coast some ships loaded with government clerks, broken-down noblemen, artisans, priests, and soldiers. Among them there were many rascals, a lot of greedy adventurers, and criminals condemned to exile. They brought no women, and what happened next was only too natural. Interbreeding between Portuguese and Indian women started. The first fire was lit under the Brazilian melting pot.

Today we know that many of the first white colonists to come to Brazil were Portuguese Jews who had left Portugal to escape the persecutions of the Inquisition. They were enterprising fellows not much concerned with earning money. What they had in mind was to build a safe home for themselves and for their offspring. They founded many settlements and started agriculture in Brazil. Their descendants are nowadays legion throughout the country. That is why I smile when I hear all that silly bunkum about racial purity. And that is why I smile again when you call Latin Americans a people who have in their veins all kinds of non-Latin blood: Indian, Jewish, Dutch, Moorish, Negro, German. . . .

The Brazilian social organization in the sixteenth century was feudal. The country was divided, rather empirically, into several provinces called *capitanias,* which were donated as fiefs to bankrupt Portuguese fidalgos who were to rule them as their captains. Only two of those *capitanias* prospered: Pernambuco and São Vicente. The most important figures of the Brazilian society of the period were the *senhores de engenho,* the owners of the sugar mills. They were like feudal barons who administered justice according to their whims and interests. Many of them were cruel and selfish. Their sugar cane plantations prospered and, when Europe started consuming sugar, they had a wonderful market for their product, and that meant wealth. But the landlords had to face soon a very serious problem: they badly needed workers for the plantations. The Indians were lazy and refused to go to work. I don't blame them. They loved the free loafing life under the sun; they had been happy and carefree before the coming of the white conquistadors.

The plantation lords decided to send for Negroes from Africa, and slavery began in Brazil. I need not recall what it meant in terms of horror, misery, and pain. The story of human cruelty is the same in all places and with all races. You know all about it. The rich *senhores de engenho* seemed to have no moral problems. They were growing rich; they were sending their sons to study law in Portugal; they now had big comfortable houses, and lived in luxury; they had a plentiful table, and their wives and daughters displayed silk dresses and sparkling jewels. I am sure that if I remind you that, in this very century of progress and culture, there are in old civilized Europe entire white populations reduced to the most degrading and cruel kind of slavery by a race that boasts of being the cream of the human kind—well, I am sure you will understand and even forgive the Brazilian landlords of the sixteenth century.

The Negroes entered the melting pot. It was a dark element in the already dusky mixture. The crossing between Portuguese and Negro produced the mulatto. The marriage between Indians and Negroes originated the *cafuso*. There were scattered all over the seaboard the mamelucos, the result of the mixture of Portuguese and Indian blood. The melting pot was boiling and bubbling very actively.

But what about the language? Derived from a synthetic language, Portuguese is, notwithstanding, an analytic one. It is very flexible, sonorous, and rich. It has a rather complicated syntax, many irregular verbs, and it is the only language in the world, as far as I am informed, that can boast (I am not sure "boast" should be the word) of having a *personal infinitive*. In Brazil, Portuguese was enriched with Indian words designating mainly things related with geography, fauna, flora, war, and weapons, and with African words concerning kitchen utensils, dishes, and things belonging to the realm of black magic, superstition, and the mysterious religions of Africa. The meaning of many words was changed in the new land. There were some mutilations, too, due to the difficulty Negroes and Indians found in re-producing the sounds of that European language. And lazi-ness was responsible for the suppression of many letters.

Another important human element loomed on the horizon of that colonial society. It was the Jesuit priests. They came from Spain to catechize the Indians, whose idiom they learned. They were patient, brave, and enduring. Many times those dark-clad missionaries had to face the *senhores de engenho* to plead for the poor savages. Most often they had to oppose the white men because of their cruelty toward the Negroes and the Indians.

I am expected to give you an outline of Brazilian literature. Yes, but in the sixteenth century there was no Brazilian literature at all. There were, of course, many letters, essays, and poems written on Brazil by Portuguese and foreign writers. Anyway let us not forget that little young Spanish Jesuit named José de Anchieta, who was all the time risking his own life among the ferocious cannibalistic Indian tribes and who during his leisure time used to write sweet and pure poems to Mary the Virgin. Sometimes he wrote the verses with a stick on the white sands of the beach, to memorize them. When he went away the waves washed the words out, and there was the brave unassuming man, in his black tunic, preaching again to the Indians in their own language or teaching them the parts they were to perform in the religious plays. As a poet Anchieta was undoubtedly mediocre. But he was so sincere, and so amazing is the fact of a man having the nerve and freshness of mind to write a naïve sort of poetry amid such a terrific strife, that one doesn't hesitate to consider him the first Brazilian writer, chronologically.

The first written document about Brazil is the delicious letter that Pero Vaz de Caminha, the notary of the discovering fleet, sent to his Majesty the King of Portugal. According to his most optimistic estimate the coast of the new land might be about twenty leagues long. And the way he describes in his classic prose the nudity of the Indian women is a mixture of candor and cynicism, mockery and seriousness. There is in that historical letter a passage that time and events have made famous. It is the one in which the writer tells his king that "the land is so good that, if you plant, anything will grow there." If you plant—that was the trouble. The Indian was lazy, and so were the mestizos. Of course the landlords bought Negro slaves and, under the menacing whip, compelled them to plant and to pick. But soon the men born in Brazil would be infected with the gold fever, and with the idea that to discover a gold mine or a big diamond was a much quicker way of becoming rich than to plow the land and wait for a problematic harvest. The land is so good . . . yes, in a way that was a sort of curse. For many generations Brazilians relied too much on the words of the *escrivão*. And they slept, lulled by the idea of plenty and bounty in that wonderful land where anything would grow easily and richly—only *if* you planted. . . .

If we are to study the literature of a country we must not forget the following factors: race, environment, and historical time. But may I say: "Tell me what blood you have in your veins, the place where you live, and the precise time you did your writing, and I will tell you exactly what kind of literature you produced"? Of course not. I believe in the influence of blood and of literary fashions; I am sure of the importance of the climate and even of the shape and color of the landscape we have before our eyes. But there is something more: the individual, and a mysterious and indescribable element for which I find no name.

Brazil has three climatic zones. The largest is tropical or

torrid, and covers about six-tenths of the whole territory. The subtropical zone corresponds to three-tenths, and the temperate zone is no larger than one-tenth of the total area of the country. Brazil has all kinds of landscape: jungle, prairies, rolling fields, plateaus, deserts, big mountains. . . . And, if we examine intently the books which are written nowadays in my country, we shall notice that each region, just as in the United States, has a different kind of literature that depends somewhat upon climate, tradition, race, landscape, and even upon the kind of economic activity of each section.

Vianna-Moog, one of our most brilliant essayists, wrote that literarily Brazil is not a continent but an archipelago in which he discerns at least seven different islands, each with its peculiar intellectual climate and landscape. Many critics disagreed violently with him, because they discovered in those very islands many writers who did not fit into the picture. Well, I think myself that Vianna-Moog is "more or less" right. His method, even if it is not absolute (and what *is* absolute?), serves at least as a very clever starting point to study separately the Brazilian literary scenery, giving each region its human and artistic meaning.

But let us go back to the sixteenth century, to the melting pot where there was a race in the making. What did that mixture of Indian, Portuguese, and Negro blood mean in terms of trends, passions, psychological traits, qualities, and defects? The Portuguese contributed with the simplicity of their brave and good souls, with their almost mulish pertinacity, and with that romantic feeling they express in a word that has no correspondent in other languages: *saudade*. To feel *saudade* is to miss or to long for somebody or something; it is to be homesick, nostalgic. Sometimes Portuguese, as well as Brazilians, feel *saudade* even of a person they have never seen or of a place they have never been to. The national Portuguese song, the *fado,* is a sad music with melancholy lyrics. Sorrow is the keynote of the Portuguese poetry. As to the Indians—they were sensual and lazy, imaginative and mischievous. The Negroes brought into the melting pot the mournful music and the sense of rhythm of their suffering souls, their cosmic terror and all the ghosts of the African jungle. The "darkies" had a great influence in the Brazilian colonial society. The mammies nursed the children of the fidalgos and landlords. The Negro boys served as pages to their masters' sons. They were like dark cupids, who ran love errands, and most often they served as ghost-serenaders, singing in the moonlight with their velvet voices passionate songs under the windows of the white *senhoritas.* The mammies told the white boys and girls stories and fables of the African forests. Some of the old medieval tales and legends brought by the Portuguese were retold and disfigured by the Negresses, who lent them an African tang. Superstition was little by little being instilled into the soul of the Brazilian younger generation.

A study of the Brazilian folklore is in many ways very illuminating. It may provide us with a magic window open strategically on the Brazilian literary scene of yesterday as well as of today.

Let us take first the popular poetry. We find in it two main trends: one melancholy and the other frolicsome. At times they alternate in the same poem, in the same quatrain. I wish I could translate into English some Brazilian quatrains. Unfortunately I was never able to versify even in my own native language.

The words you find most frequently in the Brazilian popular poetry are: fate, pain, love, sorrow, misfortune, suffering, and tears. I remember one quatrain that says that chance is like a woman, because when she wants us we don't care; and when we do care she runs away.

"The roses," wrote an anonymous poet, "are beautiful even if their thorns hurt us, but the truth is that the roses fall and the thorns remain."

"I have seen your footsteps on the sand," sings a popular poet, "and I started thinking that your figure is so gorgeous that even your footsteps make me cry."

"Oh, little swallow perched on the branches of the palm tree," begs another bard, "please tell me where is my beloved girl, because my eyes are tired of waiting for her who never comes."

A popular philosopher states bitterly that he who says that he has suffered many kinds of evil is a liar, because there is only one real evil; that is, the evil of ever having been born.

But sometimes the predominant note in the popular verses of Brazil is gaiety and irreverence. There is a famous quatrain that says that when a man is about to travel he must pray once; when he goes to war, twice; and when he is going to be married, three times. Another verse runs like this: When a rat refuses to eat a piece of cheese, or a girl refuses a boy who proposes to her—well, the cheese is certain to be rotten and the boy to have some sort of handicap.

Since colonial times Brazilian literature has been rich in satirical poets like the Spanish Quevedo and the Portuguese Bocage. And one of the most picturesque characters of Portuguese and Brazilian folklore is a fellow named Pedro Malazarte, a kind of Portuguese version of Tyll Eulenspiegel. I think Malazarte—a name which means "bad tricks" —has a Spanish origin. He was an ever-young rascal, famous for his picaresque adventures; he was a swindler, a joker, a tremendous liar, and most of his stories are unprintable.

We find color and poetical beauty in the Indian legends. One of the most lovely legends I know is that of the origin of the night. Here it is.

In the beginning there was no night. It lay dormant in the

depths of the waters. The daughter of the Big Cobra—one of the gods of the jungle—had married a young man who was eager to have his wedding night. But the girl said: "It is not night yet." The young man replied: "There is no night, but just the day." "Well," the girl went on, "if you want me to sleep in your hammock, send for the night that is within the big river." The young man ordered his servants to go fetch the night. The Big Cobra gave the messengers the closed stone of a fruit and told them not to open it because, if they did, all things in the Universe would be lost. The servants went back to their master. But they heard strange voices within the fruit stone, and they were so curious that they opened it. All of a sudden there was night in the air. The bride, however, told the bridegroom: "They have released the night. Let us wait for the dawn." And in the deserted woods the does and lizards started running, and the leaves of the trees were changed into birds, and all things that were scattered over the surface of the river became ducks, fishes, and herons. And when the morning star appeared in the sky the bride said: "Morning is coming. I am going to divide it from night." And from a thread she made the *cojubin,* the red and white bird that announces daybreak. And with another thread she made the birds that sing at night. And when the servants came back their young master told them: "You were unfaithful and disobedient. You released the night and all things were lost." As a punishment the servants were changed into monkeys, and unto this day they people, noisily, the jungle.

Another legend tells us about a handsome Indian warrior who every night received in his hammock the visit of an Indian girl whose kisses were sweet and loving. The girl used to come only by night, because her love had a sinful nature and she did not wish the boy to know who she was. But the young warrior was anxious to discover the identity of the strange visitor, and so painted his whole body with the black resin of a wild plant; and that night, when the mysterious girl kissed him, her cheeks were spotted with black. Later on, seeing her face mirrored on the surface of a brook and realizing that the spots were indelible, the girl was so distressed and frightened that she decided to flee. She shot many arrows into the air, and they formed a ladder which she climbed and climbed until Tupan, the god of gods, changed her into the moon. That is why the white face of the moon has dark spots. And since that fateful day the Queen of the Night has never lost the habit of looking down to the mirror of the waters, to see if her face has still the frightful marks of sin.

The imagination of the natives peopled the jungle with many goblins and devils. There was the Curupira, a perverse fellow who used to lead men astray in order to suck their blood. He looked like a small Indian, with green teeth and with his feet turned backwards. There was also the Caapora or Caipora, a hairy giant with a sad face who used to appear commanding a herd of wild boars. If you met him in the jungle you had bad luck for the rest of your life. Unto this very day, when a person has bad luck, we say in Brazil: "You are *caipora*, my friend." Another goblin who is very popular is the Sací-Pererê, a kind of Brazilian counterpart of the English Puck. The Sací is a naked Negro midget who smokes a clay pipe and who has on his bald head a bright red cap. He has only one leg, a protruding stomach, and no teeth at all. He likes to frighten people, chiefly children, and to set cattle and horses into a panic.

I am sure you have heard of the Amazons, the women warriors whose tribes had no men, and of the Iara, the Indian replica of the mermaid—a beautiful creature, half woman, half fish, with long green hair and whose alluring voice led the fishermen astray in the "big river."

But the real hero of the Indian fables is the *jabotí*, a kind of small turtle. He is a quiet, slow-moving fellow with a philosophic mind. He likes to play the flute and he has a permanent feud with the jaguar. In the long run the *jabotí* wins, because he is a smart guy, because he knows how to play ball with the other animals and how to use time for his own benefit. He is weak, all right; he is a tiny creature, but he manages to defeat the beasts of the jungle because he is sly and never rushes. The moral of the Indian fables is the glorification of astuteness and cunning, and not of force, violence, or physical courage. And it is very interesting to observe that even today Brazilian hero worship does not center about the warrior, the explorer, the tough fighter, but about the Bohemian, the smart fellow. The main character of Brazilian jokes of today is the parrot, a congenial rascal— an animal version of Pedro Malazarte, kin to the *jabotí*.

There is a fable of African origin which tells us the story of the jaguar that asked the cat to teach him how to jump. In a few lessons the cat taught the jaguar all his tricks. After the last lesson they decided to take a walk together, and presently the cat, who was hungry, saw a mouse passing by and pounced on the poor little creature. The jaguar, who was hungry too, took advantage of the situation and jumped on the cat—only to have the greatest deception of his life, because the master, with the rapidity of lightning, jumped backwards, and the jaguar, missing him, fell squarely on the ground. "That is not fair," complained the big animal. "You did not teach me that trick!" The cat smiled quietly and said: "A good teacher never teaches all his tricks, my friend."

When the Brazilians talk about the *pulo do gato*, the "cat's jump," they mean the secret trick, the last resource, the final surprise.

Brazilian popular sayings are full of wisdom, cunning, and bitter experience. Not seldom they express mistrust; they have the realistic and political insight of Professor Cat. Here are some of them.

"When you find ripe oranges near the main road, it is because they are rotten or are full of wasps."

"When you are poor, even your footsteps are gloomy."

"God is grand, but the jungle is grander." This means that they trust in God, all right; but in case of danger they take to the woods, just in case . . .

Here we are at the end of the sixteenth century, rather puzzled by the baffling mixture of the Brazilian melting pot. The fire under it burns on. The land, we know, is so good that, if you plant, anything will grow there.

On the threshold of a new century we wonder what kind of literature is bound to come out of that pot. Let us wait. Time will tell.

II

Such Stuff As Nations Are Made Of

IN THE very beginning of the new century—the seventeenth
—there appeared in Portugal a book of poetry called
"Prosopopéa." It was a bad poem, a poor imitation of
Camões, and its main intention was to praise the governor of
the *capitania* of Pernambuco. The merit of the work is only
chronologic. It was the first book by a Brazilian-born writer.
That is why such a tiresome poem written toward the end
of the sixteenth century is still remembered today, being
quoted in almost all essays on Brazilian literature and having
some of its passages included in many anthologies, much to
the distress of students and teachers. There is another angle.
The author of that poem was, in Brazil, the first representative of a damnable race of writers whose chief concern is to
pay compliments to the governing people in order to get
from them all kinds of favors. They still exist nowadays, not
only in my country but all over the world. They have
fostered fascism, racism, and all those sad, silly, and tragic
isms. They have backed dictators and *caudilhos;* they sold
their pens to the devil; they prostituted literature. But why
waste time with such scribes? Let us go back to the good
old seventeenth century.

Good and old? Old, undoubtedly. But why *good?* Was it
not in that century that the Holy Inquisition killed Galileo?
And that the Thirty Years' War was fought? The seventeenth century was a time of confusion, hatred, and political
entanglement from which arose the kingdom of Prussia. And
we may say that it opened the road that was to lead to the

Franco-Prussian War, to the first World War, and incidentally to Hitler. (Well, but following the same technique
we could as well find the source of all wars in the incident
between Cain and Abel.) Maybe the seventeenth century
was not altogether bad. It gave us the "Descent from the
Cross," by Rubens, the experiments of Harvey with the
circulation of the blood, Corneille's "Cid," Pascal's
"Letters," and Milton's "Paradise Lost." And, if you don't
mind my materialistic trend, I shall point out a very significant happening in the seventeenth century which would
influence to some extent Brazilian literature. It was the
foundation of the Bank of England. But let us not anticipate
facts. . . .

Brazilian colonial society prospered the way all feudalistic
organizations generally did; that is to say, the barons were
growing richer and richer, whereas the serfs went under-
paid, underfed, underclothed—in a word, true to their condition of underdogs. The system of *capitanias* had failed, and
now the country had only one central government. Slavery
was going on beautifully, and more and more Negroes were
coming from Africa. The melting pot was boiling in-
cessantly.

Around the sugar mill owners and landlords gathered a
society that was no longer Portuguese. It was made up of the
sons and grandsons of the Portuguese, as well as of mestizos,
Negroes, and converted Indians. There were many families
where the influence of the Jesuit priests was enormous.
Many of the Negroes were by now Catholic converts; but
they mixed Catholicism with voodoo, and they transmitted
that barbaric kind of religion to the children of the white
men whom they nursed or valeted. There were in the begin-
ing of the seventeenth century two different social nuclei in

Brazil. The northeastern one, dominated by a rural aristocracy, was sedentary, agricultural, and definitely Catholic.
The other, whose center was São Vicente (now São Paulo),
was ruled chiefly by nomadic adventurers, rough fellows
with no religious faith or prejudices, whose main aim was
to discover gold, silver, precious stones, and to hunt Indians
to sell them as slaves to the seaboard plantation owners. In
contrast with the Roman splendor of the "sugar aristocracy," their life was Spartan. These daring men entered
the jungle, climbed mountains, founded settlements, followed the course of the big rivers, tracing rough maps of
the lands they explored. They went in groups called
bandeiras, "flags," and they were called *bandeirantes*. Poets
and novelists usually paint those men with the ideal colors
of unselfishness and patriotism, trying to picture them as self-
sacrificing creatures whose only desire was to render services
to the country even at the price of their own lives. I think
that is pure moonshine. Maybe there were among the
bandeirantes a few idealistic men of good will, but the
majority of them were just brave rude adventurers spurred
by the idea of becoming rich. All the same, they were
tremendously useful and did a splendid work. They expanded the frontiers of Brazil in many directions. They
founded hundreds of settlements that later became cities.
They made history, even if they did not intend to.

Classicism was reborn in Europe in the middle of the
fifteenth century, and its rather cold light flooded the whole
of the next century. But soon its marmoreal and dignified
simplicity began to bore writers. They needed something
more sophisticated. They wanted a change, and that was
the beginning of a literary fashion which dominated the
seventeenth century. In England it had the name of euphu-

ism. In France it was described with the adjective *précieux*. And as in Spain the high priest of the new school was the poet Gongora, it took there the name of gongorism.

If the classicists had as the symbol of their writing the simple straight line, and sometimes the graceful curve, the gongorists adopted as a norm the broken and the mixed one. They wrote long, long passages full of interpolated phrases which separated verbs miles and miles away from their subjects. They never said in two plain words what they could say in many twisted sentences crammed with unusual vocables and images. Some critics try to give a political explanation of gongorism, saying that the Holy Office exercised so severe a censorship on the writings of the time that the authors, to elude the Inquisition, adopted that sort of code writing in order to say what they wanted in a manner not so clearly understandable. The explanation is clever but a bit gongoristic too.

From 1580 to 1640 Portugal was under the political domination of Spain; and so it was only too natural that gongorism should influence Portuguese writers, infecting also the young Brazilians who were studying law at the University of Coimbra. Who were those young men? Just the sons of the wealthy plantation owners of Recife and Bahia. So when they went back to their country, where many of them became writers, they carried with them the seeds of gongorism, which germinated easily in Brazil. (You must not forget the land was very good.)

That is why we find in Brazil, in the seventeenth century, a kind of literature completely imitative. Bahia was the city which held the most important group of writers of the period. They used to read and follow the Italian, Spanish, and Portuguese poets of the Renaissance: Tasso, Gongora, Lope de Vega, and Gabriel de Castro. Of course not all Brazilian authors were gongorists. Many of them remained faithful to the classic ideal. Meanwhile the people had nothing to do with the kind of literature that was being produced in Brazil. The common man spoke a different language. He was no gongorist, no classicist. He knew no Latin. In their majority they were illiterate. And the "Brazilian language" by that time had already about five thousand words more than the original Portuguese. The first popular quatrains were sprouting everywhere anonymously. But it was bad taste and bad manners for a cultured man to repeat them in high society. There was no Brazilian poet or prosist bold enough to use popular words or phrases in his writings. The literati followed snobbishly the European fashions. And when they had not had the privilege of having been to the University of Coimbra, they tried at least to imitate the writing and the manners of those who came from there. One of the psychological traits of the mestizos is pedantry, and an amazing capacity for imitation. They hate to remain at the bottom step of the social ladder. They try to overcome their inferiority complex through emulation in literature as well as in manners. The Negroes, on the contrary, are more faithful to their own nature; they are rather proud of their race and standing. They keep their personalities; they do not imitate. In the case of colonial Brazil they imposed upon the white men and the mestizos their songs, music, dances, foods, and even superstitions. As to the noble Portuguese of the time—they felt *saudade* of Portugal, whose court they tried to emulate. They daydreamed with the metropolis. The Recife and Olinda society lived in the luxury and the dissipation of the Lisbon court. They drank the best of wines, held the most magnificent of banquets and balls, wore the brightest dresses and jewels. It was a picturesque small world of turmoil, and it is really a pity that no writer of the time tried to write accurately its chronicle.

During the previous century the Brazilian seaboard had

been attacked by French and English pirates. But only in 1630 did the country have to face the first real invasion. The Dutch "Company of the Western Indies" sent a powerful fleet to attack northern Brazil. Having succeeded in the second attempt, they landed in Recife. Their domination lasted about thirty years. That is why when you travel nowadays across the Brazilian backlands you sometimes find some mestizos with bronzed skins and light blue eyes or blond hair.

What did the Dutch do in Brazil? They plundered the land and the people, sending to Holland all the riches they could. Of course there were among them leaders like Maurice of Nassau who thought such a policy stupidly unwise. He had a vision of the future. He followed the tradition of Erasmus; he was tolerant and clearheaded; he knew all the time that the best thing to do was to try to consolidate the conquest with kindness and sound political measures. However, Holland was too preoccupied with draining quickly the Brazilian wealth into her treasury. But bad treatment and heavy taxes irritated the natives, who organized (maybe "organize" is not precisely the word) their armies to fight the invader. Portugal did not want to antagonize Holland. She was still very much concerned with her old and dear dream of India, and so she advised the patriots to quit fighting. The rebels did not. They adopted the guerrilla technique; they raised hell for the conquerors. And who were those Brazilian warriors? They were rich landlords as well as mestizos, Negroes, and even Indians. Why were they fighting, if the land did not belong to them, as long as they were ruled with as much ruthlessness by the Portuguese? The answer is both material and spiritual. In the first place you had the influence of the landlords and sugar mill owners whose economic interests had been affected by the Dutch domination. On the other hand you had the influence of the

Jesuit priests in the minds of the common men. The invaders
—cried out the padres—were Protestants, "sons of the
devil," and it was the duty of every good Brazilian Catholic
to fight and expel them to liberate that land which belonged
to the true religion of Christ.

The patriots fought wildly during many years. They won
a pitched battle and managed to expel the enemy from their
country. During the last years of the campaign Portugal had
decided to help the natives, but after the victory she failed
to understand that something tremendous had happened to
the Brazilians. They had suffered, toiled, fought, all of them
—white, brown, black, and copper-colored men. For the
first time they were thinking or acting in terms of a common
cause, a common flag, and a common country. That is the
stuff nations are made of.

While those dramatic scenes were being staged in the
northern part of the country, the *bandeirantes* proceeded
with their adventurous explorations. Their native towns
were poor, rustic, and dull, in contrast with the luxury of the
casas grandes of the sugar cane plantations. The *paulistas*
were busy conquering new lands, discovering gold and
silver mines, extracting diamonds. Many of them died, burnt
with fever or killed by the arrows of the Indians. Not seldom
they starved to death with their sacks full of precious stones.

Meanwhile Brazilian literature remained untouched, un-
soiled, by the rough facts of life. It had nothing to do with
those dirty wars and those drab warriors who had never
learned Latin, who ignored the European poets, and who
had no sense of beauty. In a word, the poets were playing
the Portuguese guitar while Rome burned. Their only way
to show some patriotic concern was to praise the beauties of
their native landscape. To be sure, there was a man—Friar
Vicente do Salvador—who wrote a history of Brazil in

which he gave vent to some craving for freedom, and exposed Portugal for planning to rob Brazil of her wealth. His book, however, was not published until the end of the nineteenth century. There was also Padre Antonio Vieira, a great religious preacher. His sermons were eloquent, full of the Jesuitical dialectic and sophistry, and flavored, too, with a kind of sarcastic humor. They were oftentimes true works of art, unsurpassed pieces of oratory. Vieira, like a magnificent juggler, played tricks with words and ideas. And that Portuguese-born priest, who spent almost his whole lifetime in Brazil, was likewise an unreliable and sly politician. At the time of the Dutch domination he tried to discourage the patriots in their fight and to convince Portugal that it was no use opposing the invader, that the best thing to do was to recognize the Dutch rule in Pernambuco and to sign a peace treaty with Holland.

One of the very first Brazilian-born poets was Botelho de Oliveira. He was a gongorist and his best or, rather, his least tiresome work is "The Tide Island," a poem in which he gives rhyme and rhythm to a long inventory of the natural beauties of Bahia. In one of his verses he informs the reader that Bahia had four wonderful things whose names began with A: "*árvores, açucar, águas* e *ares*." Unfortunately that ancient regrettable incident in the Tower of Babel spoils the Brazilian poet's pun, because those remarkable things whose names in Portuguese began with A are in English: "*trees, sugar, waters,* and *air*."

The most important figure in Brazilian literature in the seventeenth century was Gregório de Mattos. I don't mean he has written really magnificent and immortal compositions. My admiration for him is due principally to the fighting quality of his writings and to the very nature of his soul, representative of the trends, defects, and qualities of that race in the making. To me Gregório de Mattos is a kind of symbol. As a poet he was a satirist as well as a lyricist and a moralist. He was said to have not only imitated but also plagiarized Quevedo and Gongora. He could not escape his times. But in the long run he freed his art from those influences. He was the first native voice to be heard in Brazilian literature, the first writer to use some national slang in his poetry and to translate into poetic language some of the feeling of the people—chiefly when he satirized the "rascals of Portugal," exposing the Portuguese fidalgos for their grafting, vanity, and stupidity.

Gregório de Mattos studied law in Coimbra, and he came back to Brazil only when he was in his forties. He was carefree and hard-boiled. He loved satire and nothing was sacred for him. He was constantly having arguments and being sued for libeling important people in Bahia, where he lived. He married a widow, but he had no real calling for married life and, being a hopeless Bohemian, he caused his wife to elope with another man. The *jabotí*, the small turtle of the Indian fables, played the flute. Gregório played the guitar. But the difference between these two amazing characters is that the tiny animal was quiet and peace-loving, whereas the guitar player was unrestful and quarrelsome. People called him *boca do inferno*, which means "hell's mouth." Everybody feared him. However, sometimes Gregório ceased to be ironic, aggressive, or jesting, and turned lyrical. That is why I think he is a true representative of the Brazilian soul, his mind being a territory where *saudade* and irreverence, wild joy and melancholy, dwelt together in a continuous shifting of planes.

He used to write with ease, charm, and exuberance. One of his quatrains runs like this: "The Brazilians are fools because they are all the time toiling to feed those Portuguese rascals." Here is another one: "In Brazil nobility is not a question of blood or good manners, but it depends on having money to buy compliments and flattering words." I think that such words are equivalent to political as well as literary rebellion. To begin with, Gregório de Mattos' verses—the last ones, I mean—are almost completely free from the classic or gongorist influences. They are simple, informal, and bold. They speak the language of the people.

Gregório de Mattos died at sixty-three; and it is said that in his last moments he was reconciled to the Church and, just before passing, he set his eyes on a crucifix, murmuring a sonnet he had made to his Savior which ends thus: "O Lord, Your love and my sins are very great; but all sin must have an end, whereas Your love is unending. That is why, no matter how great my sins may be, I expect to be saved in Your love."

III

Trouble in Arcadia

Wɪᴛʜ the defeat of the Dutch the so-called "cycle of defense" was ended in Brazil, and the "cycle of expansion" began. The *bandeiras* were more active than ever before and, having discovered gold, they contributed to the change in the entire life of the nation. There was a gold rush toward the central and western part of the land and, as a result of such a migration, the political and economic center of Brazil was dislocated from the north to the province that for too obvious reasons was to be called Minas Gerais, "general mines." Thousands and thousands of workers and landlords abandoned the seaboard plantations and villages, dreaming of the discovery of gold mines or diamonds. Sugar prices fell in the European markets, and that meant bankruptcy for many sugar mill owners. From all parts of the country large groups of men—white men, mulattos, mestizos, curibocas, mamelucos—came to the gold regions, like steel filings attracted by a powerful magnet. Boom villages sprouted everywhere in the gold and diamond districts. A new kind of society was born around the mines. Minas Gerais was the most important of the gold provinces. In a short while its main city of Villa Rica had about one hundred thousand inhabitants. It was the most lively of all Brazilian centers. From Bahia and from the northeast the cattle came in rafts and rough boats down the San Francisco River, which crosses many important provinces with such a providential course that it is today known as the "river of national unity."

The prosperity brought by gold to that part of the

country made it possible for Rio de Janeiro to be the capital city of Brazil. It provided also a concentration of capital and riches that later on would finance the establishment of the large coffee plantations and industrial plants in São Paulo. That is why—a very different picture from that of the colonial period—today the southern part of Brazil is the most heavily industrialized, and has the highest living standard.

During the seventeenth century the Renaissance had originated in many European countries the classic fashion of the literary academies. But not until 1724 did their reflection reach the Brazilian intellectual mirror. Many of these *academias* were founded in Rio and Bahia. They had queer names: Academy of the Forgotten Men, Academy of the Selected Ones, Academy of the Happy Ones, Academy of the Reborn. What did the academicians do? They gathered to read papers, to recite poems, and to give one another gorgeous bouquets made with the artificial flowers of eulogy and flattery. One of the academicians wrote that "our Portuguese America (and chiefly the province of Bahia) can compete with Italy and Greece in the production of clever men"—because, he added, "the carat of the gold of their talents is higher than the carat of the gold of its mines."

The gongorist influence still persisted and the shadow of Camões still obsessed many of the poets of the period. When critics write about the first twenty years of the eighteenth century they generally give some prominence to the "History of Portuguese America," written rather tiresomely by Rocha Pitta, and to "The Island of Itaparica," a descriptive poem from the dull pen of Friar Santa Maria Itaparica. But in my opinion the most interesting literary figure of the time was Antonio José da Silva, the Jew, who lived almost the whole of his life in Portugal. Like Gregório de Mattos, he was a satirist. He used to write plays which were staged in Lisbon, and which were very popular at that. They were farcical plays, in the *ridendo castigat mores* vein. His first work had the title "The Story of the Great Don Quijote de la Mancha and of the Fat Sancho Panza." It was a real hit. Silva's comedies were generally ironic, and they exposed the stupidity of the Portuguese nobility as well as the ignorance of the people. They were funny according to the patterns of the time, and their humor most often was rough and revealed a very bad taste. But—heavens!—those plays meant something as social criticism and as comedies of manners. The author mixed in them much of the Italian opera with the Spanish *comedia*. There was almost always a character who acted as the mouthpiece of the people. He was the representative of comon sense, and in a way he was the equivalent of the chorus in the Greek tragedy. Antonio José was somewhat influenced by Metastasio's *canzonette*, and at least one of his plays reminds us of Molière's comedies.

It is amazing and at the same time depressing how history repeats itself with the fateful regularity of a tragic ballad. The Inquisition, deciding that Antonio José as a playwright *and* a Jew was a dangerous fellow, arrested him and, after compelling him to swear he would turn a good Christian, released the poor creature with both hands maimed. But Antonio José went on writing in the same vein, and his plays went on meeting with the greatest popularity. The Holy Inquisitor was so concerned with the salvation of the Jew's soul that he burnt his body to death in a public square. But the gods took revenge. Unto this day they have never allowed a first-rate theatrical literature to arise in Portugal. And the curse seems to have somewhat reached Brazil too.

The eighteenth century was a wonderful epoch. Rousseau with his "Social Contract" and Diderot with his "Encyclopedia" were paving the way which would lead to the French Revolution. Goethe wrote "Werther." The United States attained its independence. Watt invented the steam machine.

Montgolfier experimented with aerostats (and the world went on ignoring an unassuming Brazilian friar, Bartholomeu de Gusmão, who more than seventy years before had performed successfully the same kind of experiments). Then there came the French Revolution. Diderot used to say that "freedom seems to be the spirit of our century." Writers and artists were beginning to react against classicism and gongorism. They were falling in love with nature, turning their eyes lyrically to the noble savage. They praised the shepherds and their rustic life. They painted country landscapes; wrote verses full of dewy meads, murmuring brooks, nymphs, and sweet-smelling flowers. Rousseau invited the people to go back to good old Mother Nature, and Voltaire declared that when he read Rousseau he felt like walking on all fours. Tired of so much elaboration and stylistic complication, writers took to simplicity. When they gathered it was no longer in pompous academies, but in Arcadias—a name they borrowed from a province of ancient Greece whose inhabitants cultivated music and poetry. The first Arcadia had been founded in Italy, at the end of the seventeenth century, and toward the middle of the next century Brazilian poets and prosists began to go Arcadian via the University of Coimbra.

The most important cultural center of Brazil in the eighteenth century was Villa Rica, in Minas Gerais, where a kind of aristocracy—based on gold and diamonds and no longer on the sugar cane—was beginning to take shape. Huge fortunes were made overnight. It was natural that Villa Rica should have then the most brilliant group of men of letters, because the city was the real capital of the country. It was there, too, that a remarkable sculptor unassumingly made his appearance. He was a poor crippled little man, Antonio Francisco Lisboa, nicknamed the Aleijadinho. Since he had no hands, he used to have the hammer and the chisel tied with ribbons to his wrists; and so he painfully carved the stone, giving it the shape of angels and saints and leaving on the face of those images the marks of his suffering soul. Many of the Minas Gerais churches keep still the sculptures of the Aleijadinho. The faces of his saints remind us—or rather *me*—of the tortured features of Van Gogh's figures.

But that was not at all a happy and quiet society. There were hatred, lust for gold, and violence in its foundations. Portugal kept a whole army of representatives, fiscals, tax collectors, and soldiers around the mines. The Brazilians hated them. They knew they were toiling to pay for the luxury of the Portuguese court. Meanwhile Portugal was receiving more gold and precious stones than she had dreamt of in her wildest Oriental dreams. And such a golden flow was to change the political and economic life of the country. Prices went high because gold went down in consequence of its accumulation. On the other hand Portugal, who had a feud with Spain, sought the protection of England. Both nations signed a treaty according to which Portugal was to remain an agricultural country and to let English clothes and other manufactured woolen products enter her ports freely. From that day on, Portugal was doomed to live in the shadow of Great Britain. And it is easy to understand how life would be in a new and agitated country which was compelled to live in the shadow of Portugal, whose thirst for gold seemed to be unquenchable.

Some of the poets of Minas Gerais had read the French encyclopedists. They let themselves be lulled by a noble dream: to free their country from Portuguese domination. They conspired. But, you know, it was a conspiracy of poets. They did not realize that they had to have the support of the people to make such a revolution successful, and you cannot count on the people unless they are starving. That was not the case in Villa Rica and in the surrounding districts. Gold dazzled their inhabitants. Those who were not already rich were intoxicated with the idea of becoming millionaires the next day. They did not care much for political freedom. The majority did not even know what such words meant. The conspiracy failed. Its head, a brave man, Joaquim José da Silva Xavier, was condemned to death. The poets were arrested, and some of them deported.

One of the most important literary features of the eighteenth century was a group of poets known as "Escola Mineira." Who were they? To begin with, there was Santa Rita Durão, a poet influenced by Camões, whose most remarkable work is "Caramurú," a poem in ten cantos. It is a narrative poem, rather dull and conventional. Its main merit is that it has as subject a Brazilian story, a Brazilian setting, and Brazilian characters. There was another epic poet, Basilio da Gama, whose "Uruguai" is considered to be the most important poem written during the whole colonial period of Brazil. It describes the war between the Indians and the Portuguese in the Jesuit missions of the Uruguai River. It is really a Brazilian epic. It has pomp, grandeur, and a kind of severe beauty. Basilio da Gama did not imitate Camões and he must be considered a pioneer in the field of Indianism, which was to come in the second half of the next century as one of the aspects of romanticism.

Claudio Manoel da Costa studied law in Coimbra, traveled largely in Europe, and went Arcadian. His poetry is far from being spontaneous. He was rather a clever and cultured technician of verse. The other poets of the group were Arcadian too. One of them, Silva Alvarenga, may be regarded as a transitional figure between Arcadianism and romanticism. As a matter of fact, almost all the six poets of the "Escola Mineira" had a romantic flavor—as long as they were Arcadian. If you exclude the first two epic bards, the others had nothing more left of the classic tang. They were lyric, sentimental, and more preoccupied with feelings than with form. Thomaz Antonio Gonzaga is chiefly known as the author of the most inspired love poems in the Portuguese language. Having studied in Coimbra, he was in his middle thirties when he came back to Brazil. He fell in love at first sight with a young lady named Maria Dorothea. "As soon as I saw your face," he wrote in a verse, "my blood froze, my tongue was tied, and my cheeks grew paler." Gonzaga started writing passionate poems to the beloved *senhorita*. And, as he was an Arcadian, he chose as pen name that of a shepherd, Dirceu, and selected for Maria Dorothea the pleasant name of Marília. The title of his most famous book is "Marília de Dirceu." Its keynote is a rather melancholy kind of lyricism. Gonzaga was arrested as a conspirator a few days before his marriage to Marília. He was tried and ,deported to Africa, and it is said that, having lost his love and his country, he lost his mind too. His verses, notwithstanding, are still alive. They are sweet, simple, and inspired. And, if you realize the period in which they are written, you can manage to like them without restrictions.

There is a literary puzzle connected with the "Escola Mineira." In the times previous to the conspiracy there appeared an anonymous satirical book—"The Chilean Letters," a poem portraying with ferocious sarcasm the governor of the province. Some critics say that Thomaz Antonio Gonzaga wrote it. Others claim that Claudio Manoel da Costa was its real author. If you read the sad and sentimental poems of Dirceu, you can hardly picture him writing such a poisonous and harsh caricature. Maybe Da Costa is the man. Whodunit? I don't know and I don't care. All I know is that, fortunately, the Brazilian writers of the eighteenth century were beginning to be socially conscious, and to look down from the window of their ivory towers to the people and their problems.

After the episode of the "Escola Mineira" there is in the Brazilian literary scene a kind of void, a period of transition whose geographical image may be a monotonous plain. In vain you look for a mountain. Yes, but there I see a hill against the horizon which still holds faintly the sweet colors of Arcadianism. It is Mathias Ayres, a prosist, a humanist, a moralist, and a philosopher. He is the author of "Reflections on the Vanity of Men." In his most famous book he wrote that "malice is a kind of natural art made from combinations and consequences, and in such a sense malice is a political virtue." (I must parenthetically say that we Brazilians are a people endowed with malice and with political virtues, but I honestly do not believe we are a vain people.)

In that transition period between Arcadianism and romanticism, Brazil had many religious preachers. The tradition of the pompous speeches continued. People generally went to church more to listen to an eloquent sermon than out of religious motives. In some states of my country rhetoric is a kind of congenital vice. But we must not be too ironical in judging these preachers. Some of them did a wonderful work. Portugal did not allow Brazil to have her own newspapers or even printing houses. The Portuguese alleged that "there was corruption in France because of her press." They knew that the printed word was dangerous like poison, because it could disseminate as well as stimulate ideas of freedom and equality. (Even today, in the age of the cyclotron, penicillin, and television, dictators all over the world hold the same opinion of the free press.) And, since there were no theaters in those days in Brazil, the only vehicle of Brazilian ideas or, rather, ideals was the pulpit. Of course people knew by word of mouth what was going on in the city. That was the gossip column, and the news, whereas the sermons were the editorials which dealt with political and social problems. Naturally they reflected the interests of the Church; but everything was well, once Brazilian society was mainly Catholic. The Jesuit colleges were the only ones at the time. To have studied with the Jesuits was in itself a distinction for any man. And we must not forget that now—I mean at the end of the eighteenth century—there were many priests native to Brazil, and therefore contemplating the liberation of the country. And it is only fair not to forget, too, that in the many conspiracies which aimed at the independence of Brazil there were many Catholic priests among the leaders.

So we arrive at the end of one more century. Looking backwards, we see many interesting facts in Brazilian life. The wars against the invaders had awakened in the people a feeling of patriotism. The ruthlessness of the Portuguese tax collectors in the gold and diamond districts had led their inhabitants to a real craving for freedom. In a succession of wars and treaties the frontiers of the country had expanded southwards, and for that expansion, as well as for others in different directions, the nation was much indebted to the *bandeirantes*. The first seeds of rebellion from the French Revolution had started to reach Brazil, brought by young men who had studied at the University of Coimbra. The first booklets, pamphlets, and bulletins packed with revolutionary ideas began to circulate secretly. The rivalry between Brazilians and Portuguese was increasing and had originated many armed clashes. The fate of the country was foreshadowed.

As to the writers—there were among them poets who still imitated Camões, who used to write like Gongora, who boasted of being good Latinists, who were still Arcadian or irretrievably classic. But some of them were trying to proclaim the coming of age of Brazilian literature, liberating it at least from Portuguese influence. They were reading Rousseau, Chateaubriand, Diderot, and—heavens!—Voltaire.

And now, using the technique of the eighteenth century novelists, I shall anticipate that in the next chapter you will hear about an event that was to change the entire life of the country. It was the coming of Dom João of Portugal with the whole of his court to Rio de Janeiro. For that regal gift the Brazilians were to thank a little fellow who at that time was trying to conquer the world. Yes, Napoleon Bonaparte.

IV

"My Country Has Palm Trees"

AT THE beginning of the nineteenth century brave little Portugal was in a very bad spot—squeezed between the French, who asked her to close all her ports to the English, and her old ally and creditor, Great Britain. Dom João of Portugal tried to play ball with both contending nations, but Napoleon lost his patience and ordered General Junot to invade Portugal and to arrest her royal family. The Portuguese had no army strong enough to oppose the invaders. They knew their neighbors, the Spaniards, were already defeated and dominated by the French. So Dom João decided (or, rather, fate and England decided for him) to escape to Brazil with the whole of his court. He sent aboard the ships of the Portuguese fleet about fifteen thousand persons: ministers, magistrates, priests, noblemen with their families, soldiers, servants. . . . They took with them everything they could: money, works of art, historical relics, and all kinds of valuables. And so they went, bound for the New World, convoyed by the English fleet, which was not willing to lose sight of the royal debtor.

People in Rio de Janeiro received the king and his court with *vivas*. They understood the meaning of that arrival. Their city was to lose its colonial standing and become a real metropolis. A new life was beginning for Brazil. The first act of the king was to open Brazilian ports to the ships of all friendly nations. National economy, which hitherto had favored exclusively protectionism and monopoly, turned to free trade and the fostering of industrial enterprises. The ghost of Colbert was exorcised and that of Adam Smith conjured up to rule national financial and economic life.

England had a price for having convoyed the king to his new dwelling place. She had a pattern to impose upon Brazilian economy, in the apparently innocent form of tariffs dictated by the English textile manufacturers—naturally according to their own interests. Such a treaty on tariffs was signed between 1809 and 1810, and from that time on—for many, many years—Brazil was to depend financially on Great Britain. And it is curious enough that such a material dependence did not necessarily mean intellectual subordination, because from the beginning of the nineteenth century up to this very day the main influence on Brazilian literature has been definitely French.

Dom João VI gave the country its first press—the Imprensa Regia—a court of justice, a public library, the Bank of Brazil, a museum, and later an academy of fine arts.

Meanwhile English capital was entering the country. It was a time for enterprise and big business. Commerce flourished. Money now was circulating more abundantly.

A European writer who visited Rio de Janeiro in 1820 marveled at finding there four bookstores. The ban on printing houses had been lifted. The Royal Press published several books, and the first of them to be out was "Marília de Dirceu"—a collection of lyric poems by Thomaz Gonzaga, one of those conspirator poets who had dreamed of the liberation of their country. In 1828 there were in the Brazilian capital city fifteen newspapers, one of them in French, the "Courrier du Brésil," and another in English, the "Rio Herald." The Brazilian writers were now producing essays and articles concerned with political, philosophical, and economic problems. With the free trade of goods there came also the inevitable free trade of ideas. And the ideas the winds brought from Europe to the Brazilian shores had their main source in the French Revolution. On their way over the ocean they lost their taste of blood and violence; they were cleansed by time and space and when they reached the New World they were bright, beautiful, and pure, as well as full of promises of brotherhood, equality, and freedom. Brazilian writers absorbed them eagerly, and tried to adapt them to their native environment and to the problems of their people. Now they had newspapers to print their articles. Now they could even have their books published!

It had taken about thirty years for those ideas of freedom to reach Portugal, despite her being not so far from France—spatially speaking. Not until 1820 did the Portuguese manage to defeat absolutism and to adopt a constitution. But, as they were incurably romantic, I think they felt *saudade* of their king and urged him to come back to the fatherland. On the other hand they thought jealously that the fact of Brazil's getting so many advantages from the presence of Dom João VI was detrimental to Portugal.

Meanwhile Brazilian thinkers, statesmen, and writers were trying to oppose with all their might the idea of making their country go back to its previous colonial status. The plantation owners, the politicians, and the intellectuals united their efforts to separate Brazil from Portugal.

Some of the poets of that period were still Arcadian. Their voices were beginning to gain a strong lyrical accent, foreboding romanticism. Many of them were no longer concerned merely with beautiful words and nice rhymes; they were now giving vent to their feelings of doubt and unrest, as well as to their craving for freedom. The prosists were mainly preoccupied with political and philosophical problems, and with their articles and speeches they were helping the cause of the liberation of their people. One of the most prominent among them was José Bonifácio, a professor, a

mineralogist, a philosopher, a poet, and a moralist. Despite
his being one of the champions of the independence of his
country, many of his poems were written after the Portuguese classic patterns. But, generally speaking, the Portuguese influence was vanishing from the Brazilian literary
scene. There was an anti-Portuguese feeling in the air. People
turned rather jingoist. And among the literati there was a
tendency to ignore the University of Coimbra and the Portuguese writers, literature, and ways of life. The simplest and
quickest way to wipe out those influences was to imitate the
French.

If you ask me whether the Brazilian writers of the first
two decades of the nineteenth century were brilliant, I will
answer that they were useful. They lived in a transitional
period of turmoil. They had a big task ahead. There was no
time for being bright or delightful. They were not making
works of art, but history. And they proved to be equal to
their times.

The sermons of Mont' Alverne, a friar and a religious
speaker who had many disciples, were famous. His technique was that of the eighteenth century orators. He was
hyperbolic, melodramatic, and sometimes meaningless. He
used to stud his speeches with quotations from European
philosophers to impress the audience, giving them a sense of
wisdom and depth. It is generally admitted that Mont' Alverne introduced in Brazil the study of German, French,
and British philosophers. (Here I must say that even today
it is a very good thing for any writer in Brazil to quote once
in a while foreign philosophers, because critics give them
credit for that and readers gasp admiringly.)

When I was a schoolboy I could not avoid a feeling of
fear and strangeness whenever I looked at the portrait of
the Marquis of Maricá. His face was stony and stern, his
head triangular; his eyes were deep-set and black, and his

lips thin and tight. Even now, looking at his portrait, I manage to recapture in a mild way that almost eerie feeling. But something very different happens when I read today his sayings, thoughts, and reflections—so famous at the time they were written. They sound silly, even the best ones. It is said, however, that one day the marquis was furious because somebody compared him to La Rochefoucauld, whom he certainly considered a second- or third-rate thinker. Let me give you some samples of the marquis' wit and wisdom. Here they are.

"It is better to be envied than pitied."

"A dissipated youth makes a provision of ailments for old age."

"Reality never fulfills the promises of imagination."

"A bad head wrecks the whole body."

"Poverty does not provoke any envy: it is the only advantage I discover in it."

"Reading without reflecting is the same thing as eating without digesting."

"A weak government causes ambitious and rebellious people to grow strong."

Yes, let us take the cue. *Weak governments.* . . . As soon as the all-clear signal sounded in Portugal, King Don João VI decided to go back to Lisbon—leaving in Brazil as Regent Prince his son Pedro. Pedro was a grand fellow, at least from the fiction writer's angle. In many respects he may be considered a symbol of the Brazilian people. He was sentimental, impulsive, romantic, sensual, and spoiled. He was only twenty-three when his father left in his inexperienced and nervous hands that hot potato. Nevertheless, the young man did not throw it away. He held it bravely; as a matter of fact, he ate it rather voraciously. The situation was very critical. The king had taken with him to Portugal a lot of gold. Brazilian economy had a collapse. The commercial activities decreased suddenly. There was in the air a feeling of distrust, unrest, and impending disaster. "What is going to happen next?" everybody asked. People were excited. On the one hand there were the Portuguese merchants, who felt helpless when they saw vanishing on the horizon the ship which carried their king back to Portugal. On the other hand you had the men native to Brazil, who formed a strong party and who were trying to get the young prince for their side.

Time passed. From Lisbon, Dom João VI took several measures to prevent Brazil from attaining her independence. He knew very well his fiery son: sooner or later his romantic nature would throw him into the arms of the Brazilian partisans. "Come home, Pedro!" he commanded. But the prince, urged by the Brazilians to stay in the country, disobeyed his royal father and stayed. Later on, Dom João VI, in a series of absurd decrees, tried to weaken Brazil by dividing its provinces. Irritated by those decrees, warmed by the support of the native patriots, Pedro decided to proclaim the independence of Brazil. Beside a brook, in the province of São Paulo, on September 7, 1822 (so we learn in school), the prince raised his sword and cried out: "Independence or death!" But some exacting and realistic historians affirm that his gesture was not so romantic nor his words so heroic, the real historical phrase being unprintable. That may be true. The prince was no poseur. He had much of Pedro Malazarte, of the *jabotí*, and of Gregório de Mattos.

Anyway, Brazil was free. Her patriarchs gave her a constitution modeled after the French one. The resistance of the Portuguese troops was not too strong. Soon they were compelled to leave the country. And the young prince, now Dom Pedro I, Emperor of Brazil, started eating his hot potato. Let us leave him in that rather prosaic attitude, and proceed to the period of romanticism.

Romanticism was spreading all over Europe. In France it was the latest fashion, fostered by such writers as Chateaubriand and Madame de Staël. Of course romanticism had originated in the last twenty years of the previous century in Germany, with Schlegel, Klopstock, Goethe, and Schiller. The French at that time were too much absorbed with their revolution and later with Napoleon's adventures to pay any attention to simple literary facts. But now the Napoleonic empire had ended, and the dominating bourgeoisie found out that romanticism was the real stuff for their palates. They were sentimental, simple-minded fellows. They had no use for classicism—that was an aristocratic attitude toward life. They had defeated the aristocracy. Well, long live romanticism! The very constitution that had arisen over the dead body of absolutism spoke a romantic language. The words liberty, equality, and humanity had a most romantic flavor. Besides, romanticism was a realm wide enough to shelter all kinds of souls and dreams. It had no rigid boundaries, no strict code. It could mean a flight from the Dark Ages as well as a return to them. It could mean the repudiation of religion as well as a coming back to the Church. Romanticism offered a literary and artistic pattern for those who were not satisfied with reality, as well as for those who thought that classicism was a too inhuman attitude toward that same reality. It was the victory of fantasy over reason. Aristocratic writers had been all those years talking and writing about differences in blood, and placing nobility in questions of birth. Romanticism, however, affirmed that all men were naturally good, even the savage—nay!—especially the savage, according to Rousseau. But the keynote of romanticism was not wild joy or the simple contentment of folks at peace with earth and sky. It was sorrow, melancholy, doubt, and sometimes despair. It was "*le mal du siècle.*"

In my opinion romanticism was a garment especially made for the Brazilian soul. It fitted it like a glove. Now poets and prosists were allowed to tell their readers all about their sufferings, doubts, and passions. They could describe the features of their beloved ones and even make them more beautiful than they really were. They could lend color and glory and a universal meaning to their own ailments, especially when they had some lung disease.

The first romantic poems to be written by a Brazilian were those which José Bonifácio sent from Europe, where he was exiled. However, Gonçalves de Magalhães is generally considered the first Brazilian romantic poet. His verses had a rather mystic flavor, and the title of his first book gives us an idea of the general poetic feeling of the time. It was called "Poetical Sighs." The form of its poems, notwithstanding, had still some vestiges of classicism, but their subject and their emotion were most decidedly romantic.

In Alvares de Azevedo we detect clearly the influence of Byron, Shelley, Leopardi, and Musset. The following verse gives you an idea of his literary predilections.

> *At my bedside my poets sleep*
> *All confused upon the table:*
> *Dante, the Bible, Shakespeare, Byron. . . .*

Alvares de Azevedo is known in Brazilian literature as the "poet of doubt." The shadow of death darkens almost all of his poems. He wrote a melancholy farewell to life in one of his most famous poems. He asked to have his body buried in a forgotten forest, in the shadow of a cross. As an epitaph he suggested these simple words: "He was a poet, he had dreams, and he loved."

The most significant poet of the first period of romanticism in Brazil was Gonçalves Dias, who fell in love with nature and the natives—becoming Indianist. His verses, even when lyric, had a more masculine touch than those of his contemporaries. He chanted the feats of the Indian warriors. He described passionately the beauties of the land. There was no joy or elation in his descriptions of the Brazilian landscape, but rather a nostalgic quality—maybe a premonition of the exile that would befall him. His "Song of Exile" is.one of the most popular poems of Brazilian romanticism. The poet wrote:

My country has palm trees, where the sabía sings.

In the next two verses he states that alien birds did not warble so beautifully as the Brazilian ones.

The most naïve of all Brazilian poets of the romantic group was Casemiro de Abreu, whose sweet poems were usually recited at the provincial evening parties by pale and romantic-looking young men, and by sweet and enraptured girls who gave their voices a dramatic intonation, while some melancholy person played softly at the piano a becoming accompanying melody, which in most cases happened to be the one known by the name of "Delilah." Oh, good old times of peace and good will! No radios. No airplanes. No air raids. No propaganda. No Goebbels. Just people—plain people who believed in the natural goodness of mankind, and who cried quietly when they read or heard Casemiro de Abreu's verses in which he complained about feeling *saudade* for the time when he was eight years old—"the dawn of my life"—a happy time in which he used to run and play lightheartedly in the shadows of the banana trees.

Romantic poetics sprouted everywhere in Brazil like mildew in a damp closed room. This botanical image is not so purposeless as it may seem at first sight, because most of the poetry produced at that time in Brazil had a parasitical and rather unhealthy quality. It lacked sun, joy of living, and fresh air.

Laurindo Rabello was a great Bohemian. His verses were now gay and irreverent, now pessimistic and nostalgic, and sometimes even misanthropic like those of Junqueira Freire, a queer type, who, being unable to take hashish like Baudelaire, used to eat camphor because he thought perhaps such a habit was very suitable for a romantic poet. Fagundes Varella drank heavily, like Poe and Musset. Byron's satanism infected the souls of most of those Brazilian poets. They "enjoyed"—and "enjoy" is the exact word—a feeling that later the greatest Brazilian novelist, Machado de Assiz, would describe as the "voluptuousness of boredom." Escaping somewhat that *tedium vitae*, Porto-Alegre, one of the pioneers of romanticism in Brazil, wrote verses filled with patriotic and religious feeling. His most famous work, "Colombo," is a descriptive poem in which the poet displays some erudition and a passion for rhetoric which led him oftentimes to a mere play on beautiful words.

Gonçalves Crespo was a most remarkable poet, and I am having some difficulty in finding him a place in the romantic scene of Brazil. His poems were well made and revealed such care as regards meter and construction that he must be considered in many ways a precursor of the Parnassians. On the other hand he never sacrificed the graceful spontaneity of his verses just to please the gods of form. So let us leave him with one foot firmly set on the continent of romanticism and with the other touching lightly the marmoreal lands of Parnasse.

But the greatest figure of the whole romantic period was Castro Alves, the first of our socially conscious poets. Among the poetical works produced during that epoch I can find no other poems which can stand a rereading like those of Castro Alves. He had also a passion for words and his trend to grandiloquence was so strong that his poems were described by a critic as "condorlike," which means that their natural atmosphere was that of the verbal altitudes. But I find them always readable, and sometimes they strike me as possessing an unsurpassed grandeur. They are generally free from cheap sentimentalism and their images, far from being imitative or vulgar, are bold, new, exquisite, and sometimes remind me of—no, "remind" is not the word; they rather anticipate the technique of the symbolists. Castro Alves was not concerned only with love, sorrow, or doubt. He had human understanding and pity. He had a wonderful sense of brotherhood. While the majority of his contemporaries were poking at their own wounds, making them bleed because that gave them good motives for poetry, Castro Alves turned his eyes to the chronic and ever-bleeding wounds of the slaves and made himself the champion of abolitionism, describing in rather realistic poems the sordid drama of slavery in Brazil. In many ways his writings were prophetic. I think he may be regarded as a link between romanticism and realism. It is really disgraceful that I am not able to render into good English verse some of the gems of Castro Alves. Please let us forget about rhyme and rhythm, so that I may give you a rather disfigured sample of that poet's art.

It was a Dantesque nightmare! The deck,
Giving a red hue to the reflected glow of the lights,
Was drenched with blood! The irons tinkled! The whips
    whistled!
And legions of men, black as night, horridly danced. . . .

In a few verses Castro Alves gives us one of the most magnificent and concise descriptions of an African landscape that I have ever read in any language. I tried to translate them into English prose, but it was no use. The whole thing sounded rather like a caption from a travel agency's poster advertising a trip to sunny ancient Africa.

When France surrendered to the Prussians in 1870, Castro Alves was horrified by the "barbarism of the Huns" and invited the "sons of the New World" to raise loudly their protesting voices to overlay the horrible roar of the cannons. And he made such an invitation "in the name of progress, and in the name of the future."

In many of his poems Castro Alves anticipated the proletarian vindications that were to come many, many years later. In a Catholic country and during a romantic era in which the poets were mainly preoccupied with the color of their sweethearts' eyes or with their personal sorrows and ailments, Castro Alves did something that seems to me really amazing. In a verse he exclaimed:

> *Let us break the Pope's scepter*
> *To make of it a cross!*
> *His purple may serve to cover*
> *The bare shoulders of poor people.*

Castro Alves was the greatest of the pioneers of abolition, which was to come almost twenty years later.

Only with the romantic movement did we get our first novelists. The novel started in Brazil with Manoel de Macedo. You cannot read his books today for other purposes than mere literary curiosity, or the desire to have a glimpse of the Brazilian social life in those days. They are naïve and rather poor as regards technique, writing, and characterization. They have, however, the merit of portraying with a lovable candor the family life of the Brazilian middle class of his times. Macedo's plots are simple and movingly silly. The characters of his books are either too good or too bad in a positive manner, without any psychological shading. Their conflicts are childish, their dialogues a bit conventional, and the author's treatment of his subjects is sugary and sentimental. His stories always have a happy ending: the villain is punished; boy marries girl, and they live together in perfect happiness forever after. Macedo's books were popular until the first decade of this very century. His novels "The Fair Lad" and "A Moreninha" (*moreninha* being the diminutive for *morena*, "brunette") have a sentimental place in our literature. Almost all Brazilian novelists, poets, and critics who are now over thirty-five read and enjoyed those two books when they were sixteen or eighteen, and that prevents them from being ironical or too strict when they analyze Macedo's works today. And I must confess that I am no exception to the rule. Macedo's little brunette character was one of my first literary sweethearts.

But there was a writer who had a really remarkable inventive talent: José de Alencar. As a prose stylist he displayed a rich imagination and an amazing cleverness. I see no other writer of the Portuguese language who can match him in what concerns plot and action. You may dislike his novels, especially when you are a man of this agitated and malicious century of ours; you may find them too crammed with improbabilities, sentimentalities, and some literary platitudes. But all the same you will be fascinated by the things that happen in his stories, by their color, and sometimes by the limpidity and aquarelle beauty of his writing. Alencar was in the field of the novel what Gonçalves Dias was in the realm of poetry, an Indianist. For that he was much indebted to Chateaubriand. His "Iracema" is the story of a lovely Indian girl who fell in love with Martim, a white Portuguese warrior. She was the "virgin of the honied lips, whose hair was blacker than the wing of the grauna bird and longer than her palm tree figure." She had been born beyond, far beyond, that mountain that still looms blue on the horizon. . . . The whole book is rather a prose poem. Its story, of course, sounds artificial, but the writing is charming. In the most famous of Alencar's books, "O Guaraní," we have again a love affair, but this time a platonic one between a gallant Indian warrior and the white daughter of a rich landlord. The hero talks like an academician poet. He is noble, self-effacing, brave, and he is ever ready to sacrifice his life for the sake of his beloved. At the end of the story you see a tremendous flood splendidly described by the author. The landlord's big house is swept away by the furious waters; all or almost all its dwellers die (I am not sure about the number of casualties). But don't cry, gentle reader, because Perí, the Indian, is a kind of precursor of Flash Gordon or Superman. He manages to save his *senhorita* and they are now perched on the branches of a palm tree, watching the waters rise. I will let the author himself tell you the most sensational scene of his story.

" 'My God, Perí . . .' murmured the girl sweetly. Then over that vast desert of water and sky there happened something stupendous, heroic and superhuman, a magnificent scene, a sublime madness. Perí, in a desperate effort, embraced the trunk of the palm tree with his stiff arms and shook it out of its roots."

It was a titanic struggle, the author goes on, and in the end the Indian succeeded in uprooting the tree and in transforming it into a providential raft for himself and his beloved. The novel ends with these words: "And the palm tree, dragged by the impetuous torrent, was fleeing . . . and it vanished in the horizon." It was a very clever and noncommittal end. The author avoided the issue for those who thought a marriage between an Indian and a white girl impossible, and for those who would not suffer a novel to end with death for both hero and heroine.

To finish this information on José de Alencar I must add

that his "The Silver Mines" is one of the most fascinating adventure stories I have ever read, as well as a charming description of the Brazilian life in colonial times.

Lovable Bernardo Guimarães was a very sentimental novelist, and his book "Isaura the Slave" is perhaps the only prose contribution of romanticism for the cause of abolition.

The novel "Inocência" by Escragnolle Taunay was translated into many languages, including Japanese. The romanticism of this author is moderate and dignified. Taunay had French blood in his veins and he had a French education, which has perhaps helped him in checking any trend to romantic exaggeration not only in writing but also in characterization. He displays some preoccupation with the psychology of his characters, and with the laws of probability in handling the plot. As a matter of fact, plot was not so important for him as it was for Macedo and Alencar. That trait brings him close to the oncoming naturalists. "Inocência," the story of a simple-minded country girl who fell in love with a stranger against the will of her father, is filled with a restrained kind of poetry. Like Franklin Tavora, another romantic novelist, Taunay loved descriptions and followed the tradition of the *sertanistas;* that is to say, the writers who described the *sertão,* the backlands, and their inhabitants. In my opinion Taunay's masterpiece is a nonfiction book, "The Retreat of Laguna," in which he narrates the retreat, under the worst conditions, of a Brazilian army corps during the war against Paraguay. There are dignity, sobriety, and a masculine touch in the book. It has never a moment of boastful, verbose patriotism. I used to read that book in my school days, and I read it again today with the same delight and the same feeling of admiration for the author as well as for the characters of that real-life drama.

In the story of universal literature you find sometimes

books which escape their times, and which have a kind of prophetic quality. This is the case with "La Princesse de Clèves," by Madame Lafayette, in France; with Melville's "Moby Dick" in this country, and with Emily Brontë's "Wuthering Heights" in England. In Brazil the "black sheep" of the romantic era, in the field of the novel, was Manoel Antonio de Almeida. During these last five years there has been in my country a revival of interest in that writer, and many reprints have been made of his most important book—"Memories of a Militia Sergeant," in which he depicts, as a keen observer more concerned with fact than with fantasy, the life of Rio de Janeiro in the "times of the king." His method is realistic, and his approach rather malicious and droll. He had a good eye for pathos, a flair for the grotesque. His style was simple, unadorned, and objective. In brief, he had nothing much in common with the romantics.

Ronald de Carvalho, the distinguished Brazilian poet and critic, wrote that his countrymen as historians and critics were rather mediocre. He attributed their shortcomings to our lack of notion of stability and to our rather poor experience of the world and men. Our ancestors, the Portuguese, the Indians, and the Negroes, he added, were not concerned with philosophical and historical problems. We are magicians rather than logicians. We are poets and not prophets. Between words and ideas we take to the words and start playing joyfully with them. We are a people of passion rather than of reason. Oscar Wilde wrote that the sun is the enemy of thought. You know we Brazilians live in a sunny country. Of course I am generalizing. You must not forget that in the first chapter I confessed that, in giving you this outline of Brazilian literature, I would stick, even if implicitly, to the expression "more or less."

During the romantic era in Brazil our authors in the field

of biography, history, and criticism were few and not very brilliant. Among the historians I must mention Francisco Adolfo de Varnhagen, who was a tremendous worker, a true bookworm, a champion of accurate research. But his ideas were not original and his writing was somewhat tiresome.

General Couto de Magalhães studied exhaustively the Brazilian Indian in his massive work "The Savage."

The theatrical crop during the period of romanticism was very meager in Brazil. Among the few playwrights of the time only one deserves to be remembered, Martins Péna. He wrote plays of manners in which he tried to portray contemporary Brazilian society.

I think it is time to see what the emperor is doing with his potato. There he is, the poor fellow, in a very bad spot. . . .

The country was free, yes, but the Brazilians were hostile to the Portuguese. The aristocracy of the land, which was mainly Brazilian, despised the merchants, who were almost completely Portuguese. In the Assembly certain representatives of the provinces delivered angry speeches against the emperor, accusing him of letting himself be led by the advice of some Portuguese politicians. Pedro made an extreme decision: he closed the Assembly. What else would you expect from a temperamental monarch like him? The people rebelled. There were riots in many provinces, which contemplated secession. The situation was grave. The prestige of Pedro I had previously been undermined by some unpopular imperialistic wars against Brazil's southern neighbors. In the long run there was only one course for the emperor: to abdicate. And abdicate he did, in favor of his minor son. The impetuous Pedro sailed for Europe.

A regency composed of three statesmen took over the

government—only to face one of the most dangerous crises in the life of the nation. However, they managed to preserve Brazilian unity so gravely menaced. Meanwhile some parties urged the recognition of young Pedro's coming of age, and a bitter political campaign started around that idea. In 1840 the young prince was crowned Emperor of Brazil as Pedro II, and the country entered one of the longest and most peaceful and progressive epochs of its entire life.

The beginning of the second empire coincides more or less with the beginning of the romantic era. And its decline was to coincide with the arrival of naturalistic ideas in Brazil, directly from France. When I say "directly" I do not mean "immediately," because the distance which separated Paris from Rio was measurable not only in miles but in time too. In the very year in which Flaubert published his "Madame Bovary," the great landmark of naturalism, José de Alencar gave Brazilian readers the superromantic story of his brave and noble Indian in love with the white girl. And when in Brazil Casemiro de Abreu with his sweet poems was trying to give human beings angelic attributes, Charles Darwin in Europe endeavored to relate us to monkeys.

Here is something very curious to notice. Almost all the best Brazilian romantic poets died in their early twenties, and of tuberculosis.

If I were to select a phrase to be the catchword of romanticism in Brazil, I would pick up that verse by Gonçalves Dias which runs like this:

My country has palm trees. . . .

But the realistic reaction had started with Castro Alves, whose poems, despite their romantic tang, seemed already to reply: "Palm trees? Yes, but snakes and slaves too."

V

"Yes, But Snakes and Slaves Too"

Look at his portrait. His head is impressive, but in a romantic and patriarchal way. His hair is snowy white, silky, and fluttery, and a thick white beard covers his rather melancholy and pensive face. If there was fire in his eyes, and if an expression of rapture or wild determination transfigured his features, he would resemble a Biblical prophet or a conqueror. But no. This old gentleman must be a sage, an artist, an astronomer, or a poet. Maybe he is only a gentle and quiet grandfather. Let us see what is written under the picture. "Dom Pedro II, Emperor of Brazil." Well, all the same he is at heart a poet and a benevolent grandfather. And if you examine his eyes intently you will detect in them a moving expression of meekness and ill-disguised humility, as if the old man were trying to apologize for being an emperor. Am I not right? Now, do you see what I see? The gentleman is winking at you. Don't you hear his words? Listen. . . .

"Well, after all, what I really am is just a simple human being. A man in love with art, literature, and science. An old man who enjoys reading and writing poetry, and who is a personal friend of Victor Hugo. That's what I am. Don't mind my being an emperor. Don't stand on ceremony. You and I are made of the same clay, believe me. Give me your hand; let me shake it. See? Now I want to show you my beautiful collected works of Victor Hugo bound in sheepskin, each copy autographed by the author. And, if you don't mind, I would like to read to you my last sonnet. By the way, did you ever look at the moon through a telescope?

No? It's lots of fun, sonny, lots of fun." There is one thing that sounds phony in those imperial words. The old man would never use any slang in his speech. As a matter of fact, he was so alarmed by the way the romantic novelists such as Alencar and Macedo were writing that he had the famous philologist José Feliciano de Castilho brought from Portugal to lead a purist reaction against the writers who were tainting the mother language with so many Indian and African words, popular expressions, and Brazilian solecisms.

But, grammar or no grammar, Pedro de Orleans e Bragança ruled Brazil from 1840 to 1889: Latin America has never had a more democratic president than the second emperor of Brazil. Pedro II used to give public audiences; he shook hands with the man in the street; he gave titles and decorations to artists, scientists, and men of letters; he encouraged such men as Pasteur and Graham Bell; he studied Hebrew and translated into Portuguese poems by Whittier, the American poet; he enjoyed traveling through Europe, where he visited museums and art galleries, having at the same time many opportunities of meeting and making friends with celebrities. Sometimes he forgot all about Brazilian earthly problems to raise his eyes toward the skies. Was there any cabinet crisis? But, gentlemen, there is trouble in heaven too. Today there is a transit of Venus. I am worried. National problems must wait. I am looking forward to reading our astronomer's report.

There is a sort of golden legend around the figure of that lovable gentleman. It is said that one day Pedro II called on Victor Hugo, in Paris, and when both great men were earnestly conversing on poetry the French poet's little grandson entered the room noisily. "Greet his Majesty, my boy," Victor Hugo told his grandson. But the emperor shook his handsome head and replied: "No, my child, there is only one majesty in this room. It is your grandfather."

Pedro II, who fortunately had not inherited with the throne his father's wild passions and lack of balance, gave the country he ruled almost fifty years of progress and internal peace. He played the role of a moderator as regards the Brazilian political parties; he was a kind of "cotton breakwater" against which the waves of partisan passions died down, harmlessly. He gave the nation many schools, stimulated immigration, developed the Brazilian merchant fleet, and tried to organize the navy. Fifteen years after he took over the government, Brazil got her first railroads.

In Europe the Industrial Revolution had changed the face of things. A new era had started. Since the invention of the cotton gin the machine had gone a long way. The British empire was growing stronger, supported by her industries. Big fortunes were being made which would have an enormous influence on the future world, being the origin of many of the trusts and monopolies of today. And such a change in the means of production had necessarily to affect the prevalent ethical and social patterns. The new scientific discoveries and inventions cast their light (or their shadow, according to some thinkers) on the realm of philosophical ideas. Maybe the change was too rapid and people were intoxicated with the wild and proud promises science made them. Many taboos and prejudices were overthrown. Dogma was endangered by reason. To be sure, there was something really new on the ever-changing horizon of human life. Men expected to reach God or the negation of God through science. A French philosopher wrote that whenever an idea obstructed his mental horizon he declared it false. Maybe the last vestiges of the Middle Ages were now vanishing completely from the earth. But we use too easily and too inaccurately big words like "earth," "people," and "mankind." We forget oftentimes that generally those "new ideas" and ways of life never reach the people; I mean the majority of the people, the masses. They rather stay within a narrow circle of privileged men, their privilege being in terms of education, money, or both. Even today you find in this queer world of ours entire populations living according to the material and spiritual patterns of the Dark Ages. The benefits of progress are still restricted to the paying minorities. That is one of the features of our monstrously wrong social and economic system.

Many of the mechanical improvements of the nineteenth century reached Brazil only very late. We had to wait about thirty years for our first railroad, forty years for our first textile plants, and still longer for the telegraph, steamboats, and gaslight. A Brazilian admiral wrote in his memoirs that the empire had to abandon the first steamboat it had purchased just because if its engineer died nobody in the country would be able to replace him.

But, notwithstanding such a shortage of engineers, life in Brazil under the second emperor was rather happy—so writers affirm. Brazilian historians have sometimes a romantic outlook on men and events, and they generally tend to cling to superficialities. What did they see on the magnificent stage of the Brazilian empire? A good-looking, imposing, and cultured emperor who was a friend of the most distinguished European artists, scientists, and men of letters of his time. What else? Grave statesmen with side whiskers, glittering decorations, two-cornered hats, and sonorous titles; politicians who delivered eloquent speeches or wrote conspicuous books and articles in which they quoted foreign philosophers, especially the Count of Gobineau. When the temperature in Rio was too high the emperor escaped with his court to Petropolis, a neighboring mountain city cool and full of lawns, trees, and gardens. And you had, too, magnificent balls in spacious saloons with marble columns, swarming with well-dressed men and women—ambassadors, noblemen, army officers. . . . And they all waltzed gaily. As a matter of fact, the whole country seemed to happily waltz its life away. You could not find a better world, even in the Viennese operettas.

Yes, but that was only the surface of the lagoon. It was calm, blue, and gleaming. The historians of the Brazilian second empire never thought of plunging into the waters and burying their hands in the mud at the bottom. And by mud I mean the underdog, the neglected populations of the backlands, and the slaves.

As for the men of letters of that period—they seldom dreamt of the bottom of the lagoon. And when they did they saw it full of pearls, exquisite colored fishes, and a fantastic coral flora. They were sensitive only to their own suffering and misfortunes. When they happened to write about the Negro, the Indian, or the poor man, it was to describe them in terms of romance, picturesqueness, and pure fiction. They were too much in love with the birds, flowers, and trees of their native land to see what really was going on in the human landscape.

But, as I told you in the previous chapter, there was a poet, Castro Alves, who saw the slaves in a different light. He gave poetical expression to the suffering and misery of the captive Negroes, and his poems moved deeply thousands of readers throughout the country. And when the campaign for abolition started in Brazil, people were prepared to back it. That was the sentimental side of the problem. There was a political as well as an economic aspect of the question. Two main groups dominated the political scene. The moderate party favored monarchy and tradition and it had avoided the republican regime in 1822, when Prince Pedro proclaimed the independence of Brazil. Such a party was supported by the nobility of the land, the rich merchants; in brief, by all those who had invested money in "human material"—that is to say, slaves. The other party was that of the radicals, who since 1817 had been trying to give Brazil a federal republican system. They had discovered that the best way to throw down monarchy was to free the slaves, undermining the economic basis of the empire. Between both those powerful parties there stood the soft "breakwater," the emperor. He hated slavery. When he visited his distinguished European friends, all of them liberals, he felt uncomfortable for being the ruler of a country where slavery still prevailed. It is said that Pedro II refused to give decorations or titles to men whose fortunes had been made through slavery. But he dared not sign a decree freeing the Negroes, because he feared that such a measure could mean bankruptcy for the plantation owners and consequently economic trouble for the nation.

There is in Portuguese a saying about the devil becoming a saint in his old age. After having encouraged slavery, Great Britain now made herself the pioneer of abolitionism. She sent her warships to patrol the seas in order to prevent the traffic in Negroes. Anyway, for fear of the British fleet, the Brazilian slave merchants had to cease, willy-nilly, their sordid trade. But slavery went on within the country.

People in Brazil who had reading habits were passionately reading Harriet Beecher Stowe's "Uncle Tom's Cabin." Castro Alves was dead by now, but his poems still lived in his books, in newspapers and magazines, and in the memory, the heart, and the voice of the people. One statesman, who was against the liberation of the slaves, notwithstanding his being a liberal, declared that he loved his country more than he did the Negroes. By such a melodramatic phrase he meant he would rather see slavery going on than to have a civil war started in Brazil. Another politician stated candidly that to free the Negroes would be sheer cruelty because, left to themselves, they would all starve, poor devils. Brilliant fighting young tribunes like Joaquim Nabuco and Ruy Barbosa, as well as a fiery Negro speaker, son of a freed slave, José do Patrocinio, were bravely bearing the banner of abolitionism. At the same time, with the enthusiastic support of many other writers, politicians, and orators, these men were making republican propaganda. Brazil was surrounded by federal democracies. Everybody in the country liked the "old gentleman," but they thought that times had changed and that the monarchic system was old-fashioned. There was something more. The prestige of the second empire had been undermined since the war against Paraguay. The dictator of this small country, Solano Lopes, had armed his people, transformed his soldiers into fanatics, and invaded Brazil with a powerful army. But such a war, in the last analysis, had been the result of a series of unhappy interventions of the previous Brazilian governments in the affairs of the Rio de la Plata region. It was a nasty war in which Brazil had to pay a high price for victory: fifty thousand men and a waste of money beyond her means. People were discontented. The abolitionist campaign was growing stronger and stronger. Before the contending parties Pedro II watched the "children" play or, rather, fight, and once in a while he intervened as if to say kindly: "Easy, easy, boys. No fouls. Let us have fair play."

The pressure from inside and outside was too strong for the moderate party to stand. The northern plantation owners were on the verge of bankruptcy and consequently they found it was better for them to free the slaves and to pay them a diminutive salary than to give them clothes and food. And so they, too, joined the abolitionist ranks.

On May 13, 1888, the Princess Isabel, daughter of Pedro II, signed a decree freeing immediately all slaves in Brazil.

Dom Pedro was at that time in Europe, visiting his illustrious friends and famous places like Pompeii, Capri, Bologna, Florence, and Venice.

But let us set our clock back and see how Brazilian writers were influenced by the modern ideas which pervaded Europe. Flaubert's "Madame Bovary" had started a new fashion in the novel. That fashion had the name of "naturalism." It was concerned mainly with facts, instead of with fantasy. It boasted of having a scientific outlook on life and men. Its main preoccupation was the "human document." According to the French critic Brunetière, naturalism substituted empirical subjectivity for scientific objectivity. The naturalists quoted Hippolyte Taine, who had written that, man being physically a machine and mentally a theorem, vice and virtue were simple products, like vitriol and sugar.

What Flaubert aimed at in his novel was a kind of doctrinaire impersonality. He thought that the romantics were too egocentric and that in an age of scientific progress you could not go on ignoring human nature, and pretending that men were angels or elves. Chateaubriand could ignore the glycogenic function of the liver; but the modern writers had no reason at all to display the same ignorance, as long as Claude Bernard had divulged his important discoveries. After reading Proudhon, Michelet, and Quinet—the naturalists asked—could a novelist go on writing of his unhappy or happy love affairs, or of the gentle flowers of the fields? After the divulgation of Hegel's ideas, Comte's sociology, and Darwin's evolution, could the novelists insist on writing sentimental stories whose characters did not live according to the laws of biology, having in their veins Eau de Cologne instead of blood and within their chests a lump of sugar instead of a living heart?

These same questions took several years to cross the ocean

and to reach the ears of the Brazilian writers. The first of our men of letters to pay a courageous and intelligent attention to the new ideas was a man named Tobias Barreto, a mulatto, a scholar, and a fervent admirer of the German philosophers. He is said to have been the first Brazilian thinker who could read German. He raised his voice in a threat to the taboos and beliefs which still prevailed in his country. He claimed that society was not static, but dynamic. He cried out that theological myths had to be replaced by scientific verities. And as a critic he was the first to praise the first naturalistic novel to appear in Brazil—"O Mulato," by Aluizio de Azevedo.

The book is about a young man with Negro blood who strives to make his way in a society full of racial prejudices. The author is concerned with observed facts of real life. He is crude and outspoken. And if "The Mulatto" is not a great book it has at least the merit of having been the first important Brazilian novel written according to the naturalistic technique. "The Hive," by the same author, is a much better work. It is an impressive picture of life in certain sections of the Brazilian capital city, during the second empire. If that book had appeared today, the critics would certainly classify it as a "proletarian novel." The sordid and mean life of poor people is described in "The Hive" in contrast to the comfort which prevails in the house of a representative of the *carioca* bourgeoisie. But the author had no revolutionary intention in writing such a story. He saw the whole thing from the standpoint of a mere fiction writer in love with reality. In those days the propaganda novel was not yet fashionable. Of course there were the famous thesis novels, but they generally dealt with scientific, philosophic, or purely aesthetic problems. Another interesting novel by Aluizio de Azevedo is "The Boardinghouse." Like "The Hive" it is a novel of manners, extremely realistic in its approach. It is the story of a young man who comes from his northern province to try a commercial career in Rio. The life in a *carioca* boardinghouse is masterfully described by Azevedo, whose characters talk and think according to their social rank and education. The author used in all his later books a great deal of slang, which the classicists avoided and the romanticists used only in a mild and timid way.

As a writer Aluizio de Azevedo is not particularly remarkable. He did not care much about style or grammar. But his writing is vivid, sometimes picturesque and colorful, being not seldom a precise instrument for the things he wanted to say. *Beautiful* is an adjective you cannot use to describe his novels, because they are rather a faithful mirror of life—but a mirror which had an especial fondness for the ugly and grotesque side of things and human beings. Aluizio de Azevedo's "The Man," a portrait of a hysterical woman, could be classified as Freudian; the only trouble is that when the author published that book Sigmund Freud was just entering his twenties and probably utterly ignorant of his own future doctrines.

The French masters of naturalism who most strongly influenced Brazilian writers were Daudet, the brothers Goncourt, and Zola. The influence of the latter was so infectious that in Brazil he had not only disciples but imitators. The desire to follow closely in his steps was so strong that Julio Ribeiro, a distinguished writer and philologist, decided to write a novel, in the preface of which he confessed himself to be a fervent follower of the author of "L'Assomoir." He gave his book the title of "The Flesh." Some fellow writers who disliked Ribeiro used to call his novel "Meat" and to hint that, since he was so Frenchy, he should have translated his name, too, into French, signing Jules Rivière instead of Julio Ribeiro. "The Flesh," however, has magnificent passages, as regards pure writing. But on the whole it is an unconvincing piece of fiction; its characters are artificial; its situations far-fetched. The reader closes the book with the impression that the author had two main intentions when he started writing that book. The first was to exhibit his gifts as a prose stylist; the second, to prove that he too could write a novel like those of Zola.

A completely different sort of writer was Raul Pompeia, whose "Songs without Meter" suggests the influence of Nietzsche's philosophy. Just one book made Pompeia famous. It was "The Athenaeum," in which the novelist describes the life of a boy in a boarding school. Pompeia is true to life, but he is not so preoccupied with "observed facts" as is Aluizio de Azevedo. Of course he needs common, real things and events to build up a solid background for his characters. But he is concerned chiefly with the inward life of the people he creates. His writing was much better than Azevedo's. Pompeia was a rather sensitive and nervous man, very jealous of the things he wrote. When critics disagreed with him or attacked his works, he used to say of his own writings: "*Mau mas meu*," which means "Bad but mine." His life was tormented by doubt, and the world was for him full of those "black nights of the spirit" which he describes in one of his songs. Because of that, his tormented mind had no strength to go on living. And through the tragic door of suicide he entered what could very well be for his faithless soul the longest and blackest of nights. Rich in human element, pathos, and good characterization, masterfully written and well balanced, his only novel, "The Athenaeum," granted him a distinguished place in the Portuguese-language literature. It is one of the ten best Brazilian books of all time.

And now I want to tell you about our most intriguing

literary enigma. It shakes our conviction as regards the influence of race, environment, and historical time on the literary production.

Let us begin from the beginning. In the year 1839 a brown baby was born in the city of Rio de Janeiro. Well, I think an event like that has nothing extraordinary in itself. Mulatto babies are born in great quantities and in every section of Brazil every week. But that particular tiny, tanned, skinny creature who made so unpromisingly his appearance in this "vale of tears" was doomed to be, simply, one of the most remarkable Brazilian novelists not only of his times but of all times. He was baptized in the church of the suburb where his poor and modest parents lived. He received the name of Joaquim Maria—which, by the way, did not help him much. Soon his mother died and his father, later on, married another mulatto woman, Maria Inês, who took care of the boy in a very loving and maternal way. She hated so much the name of stepmother that she asked the boy to call her "godmother"—which he did very gladly, because he liked her.

Joaquim Maria grew up as all boys do, whether they are white, black, brown, or red. He went to school, he played, and he used to earn a few nickels a day selling candies from a basket along the streets. He liked to read and he wanted to learn. He had ambitions, but he had bad health and he was ugly. And the fact of having Negro blood in his veins was rather a handicap for his social ambitions, even in a country like Brazil where there is practically no race discrimination. Joaquim Maria was sixteen years old when he wrote his first poem, "To an Angel." The next year he was admitted as a typesetter apprentice in a printing house. Later on he was promoted to proofreader. He went on studying at night, and writing poetry and prose. Soon he saw his own articles, poems, and short stories published in magazines and newspapers. His financial situation grew better. He published his first book. His first three novels were written according to the patterns of romanticism, but they had something different—they were devoid of sentimentalities, and in many ways they rather heralded the powerful novelist that their author was to become.

The literary reputation of Joaquim Maria was definitely established when he published his novel "The Posthumous Memoirs of Braz Cubas." He was then thirty-six years old, happily married, and holding a good position as a government clerk. From that book on, his reputation increased steadily; and when he reached his fifties Joaquim Maria, known throughout the country as Machado de Assiz, was the most distinguished and respected figure in the Brazilian literary scene. He was urbane, discreet, and modest. He used to go late every afternoon, after leaving his office, to the Garnier bookstore, a traditional meeting place of the literati. Young writers came to him for advice and encouragement. The most famous men of letters of the time generally liked and admired Machado de Assiz, who had the reputation of being an exemplary husband as well as a first-rate *funcionário público*, a man of conservative habits, very strict in questions of schedule and method, a trifle too cold in his manners, and utterly timid and sensitive. Critics and readers who knew him personally could hardly believe he had written those books so full of characters and events which, to judge from appearances, were the very denial of the author's life and principles. And when Joaquim Maria Machado de Assiz died, essays on his life and work began to appear everywhere. That strange poet and novelist is indeed one of the most fascinating subjects that any literature can offer to an inquisitive mind.

Let us try to examine rapidly the "case" from different angles. To begin with, Machado de Assiz displayed none of the characteristics of his race. He had a sense of balance, he hated exhibitionism, he was discreet, and he abominated verbosity. In a land of eloquent extroverts, fascinated by the color and shape of surrounding things, he was an introvert without the love of eloquence or color. He took to the psychological novel and in his stories the plot is thin and unimportant, the whole thing being just a pretext for the writer to exercise his gifts as a dissector of souls. His characters often tell the reader what they think of life and men. Their views and thoughts are somber and bitter. They generally find in cynicism a cold but safe haven for their disillusioned souls.

But why was that happy and successful man a pessimist? Why are his books so caustic and sometimes so cynical? Did he not marry the girl he loved, despite the opposition of her family? Was she not loving and faithful to him? Did they not live the whole of their married life in the most perfect harmony and happiness? Did he not see glory, fame, and, in a certain way, popularity while still alive and relatively young?

"Yes" is the answer to all those questions. But you never know all about souls. Machado de Assiz had his secret sorrows. He suffered from a horrible disease. He was an epileptic. He feared the possibility of having one of his fits in the street or in any public place. He hated the idea of being a "show." And that preoccupation was a permanent torture to him. He also had a bad stammer. And he had Negro blood. He knew also that he was ugly. Think of all those handicaps and you will understand what they could have meant to a sensitive man like him.

I think we can trace a parallel between Machado de Assiz and the British novelist William Somerset Maugham. They are separated in time and space; they belong to different races, times, and environment. Somerset Maugham had a formal education. Machado de Assiz had not. Apparently they are as different as black from white. But an inferiority complex is their common denominator. Maugham wrote in his book "The Summing Up" that he had started his career in life hampered by several handicaps: he was short, he had lung disease, and he stammered. And both writers compensated for their vocal defect by writing fluently and correctly. They both have the love of clarity, simplicity, and euphony. On the other hand both are urbane, well balanced, discreet, and they share the same horror of verbosity and showy colors. Their views on life and human creatures are almost the same. And Machado de Assiz' character named Capitú, "the girl whose eyes were like those of a crooked and sly gypsy" and who in the long run betrayed her husband with his best friend—that charming girl is a remote kin to many of Somerset Maugham's feminine characters, who generally despise the delicate love of the hero to elope with the brutal villain.

Well, maybe my parallel is too far-fetched. I am sorry. But let us abandon William Somerset Maugham in the middle of the road and proceed with Machado de Assiz.

There is a little incident which gives us an idea of his susceptibility. One day, during a party, a talkative lady addressed him beamingly: "Why, Senhor Machado, they told me that you had a bad stammer. But you talk rather well. It is not as bad as they say."

The face of the writer was a stony mask when he answered: "Slanders, dear madam, just slanders. They told me that you were a very stupid person, and now I see that you are not so stupid as they say."

"The Posthumous Memoirs of Braz Cubas" is a novel written in the first person singular, by a man who is supposed to be in the "other world." He says in his preface that he wrote the book "with the pen of jesting and the ink of melancholy." It is a cynical story, and a very ironic one. However, there are no tears in the voice of the author but, rather, a sardonic kind of humor—a smile that could be described by the adjective "yellow." Braz Cubas concludes that nothing leads to nothing. He suggests that he spent his earthly life under the spell of boredom, "that solitary and morbid yellow flower with a penetrating and subtle smell." Braz Cubas discovered one day the "voluptuousness of boredom." In his opinion man is not a unity, but a "thinking erratum" . . . in a permanent change. But what for? Nobody knows. And the late author once in a while interrupts his narrative only to poke facetiously at the reader's stomach. As a kind of poor consolation he says that fortunately, when all is said and done, man is endowed with the capacity of making fun of his own torments.

Braz Cubas' morality is made up of advice like this: "The best way to compensate for a closed window is to open another, so that morality may continually ventilate our conscience."

Machado de Assiz, like Proust, liked to ponder over problems of time. He thought that time was the great modifier and destroyer of things, feelings, and persons. In a poem he tells us about a man who on Christmas night tried to recapture his sweet emotions of childhood, and to give them the form of a sonnet. He endeavored to catch the spirit of the old Christmas nights, but he could not. After a long and painful search he managed to write just a single verse: "Did Christmas change, or did I?" He used to say that the best thing that the present has is still the remembrance of things past.

When the hero (you can hardly give this title to poor weak and unhappy Bentinho) of his most human novel, "Dom Casmurro," or "Mr. Grumpy," discovers that his wife has betrayed him, he is distressed, yes, but he is puzzled too,

because he and Capitú have known each other from childhood. And Bentinho ponders and ponders, trying to find out
if she was a victim of her instinctive impulses or just a hypo-
crite. He wanted to know also if the grown-up traitor lived
potentially within the child. And he ends his melancholy
story confessing to the reader that he has had no children of
his own, and therefore "he transmitted to no one the legacy
of his misery."

His short story "The Attendant" is told in the first person
by a dying man who confesses that long ago, called to nurse
a very sick and irritable old man, he was hit violently in the
head by a bottle the invalid threw at him, and he was so
blinded with rage that he grabbed with both hands at the
creature's throat—causing his aneurysm to burst. Seeing the
old man die, the attendant was scared. But fortunately for
him nobody discovered the truth, since the sick man, according to his own physician, had been doomed to die very soon.
The attendant was haunted by remorse, and one day, much
to his amazement, he was told that the old man had made
him his only heir. The money of the deceased brought quite
a change into his life. He appeased his bad conscience by
having a beautiful marble tomb built for his victim and bene-
factor. In the long run, he managed to forget all about the
case. And now that he is about to die he feels no remorse,
and at the end of his confessions he tells the man whom he
is addressing: "If this story proves to be of any use to you,
pay me for it with a beautiful marble tomb." His last words
are a quotation from the Sermon on the Mount, but with a
verb cynically changed: "Blessed are they that *possess*, for
they shall be comforted."

In his novel "Quincas Borba," named after one of its central characters, Machado de Assiz gives us a wonderful portrait of a woman, that of Sofia. Like Capitú, "who had eyes
engulfing like a surf," Sofia is cold and sly and she fools all

the time the unhappy Rubião with her vague and never-ful-filled promises of love, while the poor man's spirit is little by little sinking into the dark sea of madness. Though not such pleasant reading as "The Posthumous Memoirs of Braz Cubas," nor so well constructed as "Mr. Grumpy," "Quincas Borba" has a magnificent psychological treatment of its characters.

But it is in the realm of the short story that Machado de Assiz was unsurpassed. His *contos* are real masterpieces which could honor any literature, past or present.

When the great Portuguese novelist Eça de Queiroz was told that the republic had been proclaimed in Brazil, the first thing he said was: "I wonder what does Machado de Assiz think of all that." But Machado de Assiz did not think at all. He took no part in the republican propaganda, as he had taken no part in the battle for abolition. He was a pure man of letters who did not care about politics or social problems.

Queer man! I read and reread his works with an ever-in-creasing admiration. His prose is rather dry, precise, and destitute of color. But it is balanced, correct, elegant, and limpid. It has a classic flavor, but all the same it is profoundly "Brazilian."

Machado de Assiz passed away in December, 1908, in his house then bereft of his loving wife, who had died some years before. He spent his last days seated in an armchair, his shoulders covered by a shawl. He suffered acute pains; but he tried not to moan or cry, because he hated to bother the good friends who visited him. When someone asked him if he wanted to see a priest to confess, he answered shyly: "I don't think so . . . it would be hypocrisy."

And there he stayed, unhappy man, seated in his chair, in the dark room, amid his memories. People came to see him, but they were not allowed to enter the sick man's room. They stayed in the parlor, whispering. One day Machado de

Assiz asked a friend: "Listen, don't you recognize those whispers? . . . It is like at a wake."

A few moments before passing, he said to his closest friend: "Life is good." And, uttering these simple words, he was identifying himself with the main character of one of his stories, a man who could hate life so strongly just because he loved it too much.

Machado de Assiz died as he had lived: composed, considerate, hating the idea of being a show or a bore and of giving trouble to his friends. Until his last moment he was faithful to his lack of faith. He was consistent, discreet, and brave.

We Brazilians are very proud of him.

VI

Wide Are Pegasus' Wings

When the general (he was an imposing man with stiff grizzled beard) entered the courtyard at the headquarters, the imperial soldiers cried out: "Long live the republic!" It was the climax of the drama. There was a moment of suspense. What was going to happen next? Were the troops faithful to the emperor going to resist? The whole thing was utterly unexpected. Of course there was republican propaganda going on among the civilian classes. And after abolition there had arisen a tremendous economic crisis: many plantation owners were bankrupt in consequence of the sudden migration of thousands of Negro workers to the seaboard cities. The liberation of the slaves had been the result of a very commendable sentimental feeling which, however, was not followed or preceded by a practical arrangement to provide the Negroes with jobs and social protection. On the other hand the aristocracy of the land had withdrawn its support from the government, in retaliation for the act of abolition. The imperial ministers had proved to be very awkward in handling the military affairs of the nation. The army officers were so discontented that the whole thing gave rise to a problem known in Brazilian history as the "military question." The structure of the empire was undermined and the people expected it to crack sooner or later, but in any case not so soon. . . .

And now General Deodoro, the leader of the army, had marched with his troops to attack the Sant' Anna Field headquarters. Another military chief supposed to be loyal to the emperor was ordered to command his men to stop the rebels; but he answered he would not fight his own brothers, and he joined the revolutionary ranks with all his soldiers. The republican idea was victorious in Brazil. Even the civilian pioneers of the movement were astounded. And so were the people—and the old emperor, who at that time was in his summer palace in the mountains. There was no shooting, no bloodshed. No! Wait a minute. . . . When the rebels told the imperial Secretary of the Navy that he was under arrest, the impulsive man's only answer was to shoot at the soldiers —who shot back, wounding him.

That eventful day was November 15, 1889. Two days later the emperor and his whole family were sent to Europe. There were no demonstrations against him. People generally liked and admired him, and those who did not at least respected that mild-looking gentleman. His last words in the letter he sent to General Deodoro were the following: " . . . and I will keep a very nostalgic remembrance of Brazil, for whose grandeur and prosperity I express my most ardent wishes." And so the emperor made his exit. And there you had the Republic of the United States of Brazil, whose new flag—a yellow lozenge against a green field, having in its center a constellated blue sphere with the legend "Order and Progress"—suggested a strong influence of the positivistic ideas which were shared by many of the Brazilian army officers.

The proclamation of the republic in my country set a very dangerous precedent. In the years to come no revolution would succeed there without the support of the whole army or at least of a part of it. Politicians generally would perform all the tricks, make the speeches, form the intrigues and the conspiracy; but the army would decide the matter when the time came for action.

But let us use the Hollywood technique of flash-backs, and take a close-up of the Brazilian poets of the three final decades of the last century. The poetical fashion contemporary with the naturalistic novel was the "Parnassian"—a name derived from the French review "Le Parnasse Contemporain," which had been published in Paris since 1866. Its contributors had decided to react against the sentimental exaggerations of the romantics, opposing their too personal and morbid kind of poetry with something more dignified and masculine. They imposed upon themselves many strict rules, and Banville, discussing poetry, wrote concerning poetic license that there must be none at all. The Parnassian credo recommended the most severe observation of the laws of meter and rhyme. It favored a rather classic attitude toward form and idea. The result of it all was in many cases impassive coldness, and generally Parnassian verses have the cool and reposeful beauty of a Greek temple. The Parnassian Jules Lemaître once wrote that he used to "polish cool and ingenious sonnets."

In Machado de Assiz and Luiz Guimarães we find in Brazil the precursors of Parnassian poetry. If you bear in mind the methodic, correct, and restrained prose of Machado de Assiz you will understand easily why the new school of poetry would have for him so great an appeal. One of his most famous sonnets, "The Vicious Circle," is to my taste just an anecdote cleverly framed in the form of a sonnet. A restless firefly, dancing in the air, said: "I wish I were that golden star." But the star looked jealously at the moon and sighed: "I wish I could be as beautiful and transparent as she." . . . "Poor thing!" moaned the moon bitterly, gazing at the sun, "I wish I had the immortal and enormous glow of the sun, to whom I owe my own light." But the sun, fed up with so much glory and splendor, looked down to the earth and murmured sadly: "Why was I not born a simple firefly?"

In the first Brazilian Parnassian poets you detect still some vestiges of romanticism. They were now stricter concerning rhyme and meter, but their feelings are rather romantic. They still shed abundant tears and they generally wrote verses about dead blonde virgins who were cold and quiet within their snowy coffins, surrounded by white roses and immaculate lilies. And they asked: "Where are you going to spend the long siesta, within that white bed of yours?" I think it is a very unusual thing to compare the journey into death with a long siesta.

After those first Parnassians, in whose verses, according to Machado de Assiz, you still smelt the "milk of romanticism," there came a very brilliant group of poets who were, so to speak, spiritual sons of Leconte de Lisle, Gautier, Proudhon, Coppée, and Heredia. The history of the Parnassian movement in Brazil may be outlined through the work of four or five of its most prominent representatives.

Raymundo Corrêa, though punctilious as regards form, was much more concerned with philosophical ideas than were most of his contemporaries. He could not escape the Brazilian national disease: he was a pessimist like Machado de Assiz. In one of his most celebrated sonnets he described the doves leaving their dovecotes, one by one, when the cool and rosy dawn breaks; in the evening they come back to their dwelling places, fluttering their white wings. Well, so far there is nothing extraordinary in the picture. But the poet suggests that the budding dreams that are nestled in our hearts fly out, one by one, just like the doves, stretching their wings—the dreams, not the doves—against the blue sky of adolescence. And they fly away. . . . However, the doves do come back to their dovecotes; but the dreams return no more to our hearts.

In "The Secret Sorrow" the same poet affirms that if people's faces could mirror all the secret anger which de-

stroys each new-born illusion, and if we could see through
the mask of their faces the pangs of their tormented spirits
—well, many persons who now cause us to envy them would
arouse pity in us instead. Because many people who laugh
have within their breasts, like a hidden enemy, a horrible
cancerous wound. And—alas!—there are many creatures
whose only happiness is to give the world the impression
that they are happy.

I think the philosophy of Raymundo Corrêa may be
summed up in a phrase of his: "Everything is pain."

Alberto de Oliveira is one of the most amazing technicians
of verse in the Portuguese language, which does not precisely mean he is its best poet. His poems do not much appeal
to me. They are too well worked out. I find no emotion in
them, just skill—the kind of skill that makes you find out a
rhyme for practically every word and that always provides
you with a way, no matter how twisted it may be, of con-
densing, in the fourteen verses of a sonnet, a story, the description of a landscape, or a philosophical idea. The first
impression you have when you read most of Oliveira's verses
is that of crookedness. His sentences never follow the direct
order. His choice of words is academic, precious, and almost
pedantic. His "Greek Cup" sounds like a literary riddle or a
mystery story. You have to read it many times to understand
what it is all about. First of all you have to discover who or
what is the subject, and where it or he or she is hidden; afterward you do your best to find out what he, she, or it did,
and when, and how. As a daring explorer who enters the
jungle and makes his way through an entanglement of lianas,
tropical flowers, thorny plants, and imposing trees, the
reader struggles in despair against the unusual vocables of
the sonnet. It is very difficult to give you in English an idea
of those typical twists of Alberto de Oliveira's poems. Let
us suppose that he wants to say that a Greek cup of gold, en-

graved by the clever hands of a goddess, one day felt tired of belonging to the same owner. . . . Now listen to how Alberto Oliveira would say the same thing in a sonnet: A engraved by a goddess' clever hands, Greek cup one day, golden, of belonging to the same owner tired felt. . . ." Here is a faint idea of what some of Alberto de Oliveira's poems are like. I suppose you would not like them. But I must say they are correct, grammatically speaking; and clever, from the standpoint of technique; and almost perfect, according to the Parnassian patterns. Alberto de Oliveira one day was proclaimed the "prince of Brazilian poets." For such a choice I am afraid the people were not responsible.

Olavo Bilac was a different kind of poet. He was not pessimistic like Raymundo Corrêa, nor so marmoreally cold as Alberto de Oliveira. He was a much more popular poet than those two colleagues of his. His verses were fluent, brilliant, sensuous, and full of passion. In four lines he condensed the supreme ideal of Parnassian art in the form of advice to poets.

> *Twist, perfect, elevate, and polish*
> *The phrase; and at last*
> *Set the rhyme on the golden verse*
> *Like a ruby.*

Bilac wrote many erotic poems. He was madly in love with the Brazilian landscape and with all women in the world, and above all he was in love with the idea of love. His work is a rich field for a Freudian harvest. His sensuality is evident not only in the subject of his verses but even in the choice of words and in the very phrasing of ideas and images. If you read Brazilian poets with some attention, you will discover in them an obsession with the idea of virginity. Their poems are filled with virginal young ladies and virginal feelings, hearts, forests, thoughts, intentions, etc.

Bilac wrote a sonnet in which he affirms that when a virgin dies a bright new star appears in the blue of the nocturnal sky. That is the reason why in the same poem he begs the lovers who wander at night along the fields, exchanging kisses and caresses, to be careful to avoid demonstrations of love, in order not to shock the little stars; that is to say, the souls of those poor creatures who have never tasted love and who died innocent. And, speaking of stars, I remember that Bilac gives us in another sonnet a dialogue between a man and his friend. One tells the other he is able to listen and understand what the stars say to him when at night he opens his window, pale with amazement, and starts conversing with them. "You are crazy!" answers the other. "What do you tell them? What do they tell you?" And the dreamy fellow confesses that only those who are in love can have ears good enough to hear and to understand the stars.

Of course those sonnets, narrated in cold prose and with a touch of irony, may seem rather ridiculous. But Bilac has written really magnificent pieces of poetry—like the long poem "The Emerald Hunter," about the adventures of one of those *bandeirante* pioneers who entered the jungle and climbed the mountains in search of precious stones. And his best verses are exactly those which are not so popular. I used to read Bilac when I was in my late teens, and I was in love with his poetry. I have reread many of his poems without managing to recapture the old spell. Now, mimicking Machado de Assiz, I ask the reader: "Did Bilac's poems change, or did I?" Maybe I did. And times changed too. The trouble is that when we try to recapture old passions or states of mind we usually look for them in a certain place—only to discover, after a fruitless search, that they do not belong with space, but with time.

Sometimes you find, in Brazilian literature, poets made famous by just one poem. That is the case with Anibal Teófilo, who spent thirteen years of his life polishing and repolishing a single sonnet, "The Stork," in which he compares a motionless stork, looking intently and longingly in the mirror of a lake, with human doubt stooping over its own infinite anguish. Another very famous sonnet is the excellent one by Vicente de Carvalho on happiness. He says that only hope, no matter how slight it may be, compensates for the pain of living; nothing more, because the whole of our life is just unfulfilled promise. And he concludes that happiness is like a tree full of golden fruit—the trouble being that it is always where we place it, but paradoxically enough we never place it where we ourselves happen to be.

The sonnet was the most popular form of poetry in Brazil at the end of the nineteenth century and in the first two decades of the twentieth.

About 1880 a group of poets gathered in Paris around Mallarmé and started writing a new kind of poetry which in the last analysis was a spiritual reaction against the cold impassibility of the Parnassians. These poets loved refined ideas and ways of literary and artistic expression. Their spiritual climate was made of faintly colored mist, agonizing twilights, and exquisite perfumes. They were more concerned with inward than with outward landscapes. They never used strong paints, but half tones. According to Mallarmé, "When you name an object you suppress three quarters of the enjoyment of the poem, which must be made of the happiness of guessing little by little; the ideal thing is just to suggest." And Verlaine, who also paid his tribute to such a school, which had the name of symbolism, used to say: "Music above all things!"

Symbolism reached Brazil in the last decade of the nineteenth century. It had not many followers in my country, where shading colors and mists are not very frequent. I must explain that the Brazilian kind of sorrow, anguish, and melancholy is rather outward. We have not many cases of introversion in our literature. Our sun is too dazzling and our trees are too green, our skies too nudely blue, not to constitute a permanent appeal to the eyes and minds of our writers and artists.

Cruz e Sousa is considered our most important symbolistic poet. He was a Negro, and he had a suffering soul. Critics call him the "black swan of symbolism." In his verses he shows an almost obsessed preoccupation with words like "obscure," "sinister," "dark," "humility," "profundity"— words that suggest shadow, prison, submerged things, underground life. I think they are perhaps an allusion to the color of his skin. And because of that horror of dark and subterraneous states of mind he was always trying to climb to luminous altitudes.

For him the path which leads to glory (he tells us in a sonnet) is a rosy and golden one, all flanked with blossoming rosebushes, laurel trees, and other equally illustrious plants. All souls are anxious to follow it to reach the fabulous treasury. And there they go, up and down, trembling and dreaming. Who are they? They are the virginal beings come from the earth, covered with the blood of a tremendous war, and they are intoxicated with the sinister wine. . . .

Like most of the symbolists, Cruz e Sousa is often almost incomprehensible. But that Negro poet had an exquisite sensibility, and not seldom the ghost of Baudelaire passes through his verses.

Alphonsus de Guimaraens was another symbolist of note. His poems had a religious and mystic touch. He loved the roses, the white lilies suggestive of long and pure hands, the ogival windows of the churches, the smell of incense, and the angels.

Forsaken love sheds tears
Within the dying heart. . . .
The leaves fall, when autumn comes,
And nobody succors them.

In another poem he narrates the death of his beloved, when "even the stars cried." The moon enveloped her with lilies and rose petals. And when her soul reached heaven, the angels, thinking of the unhappy poet who had stayed on earth all alone, asked the girl: "Why didn't you both come together?"

Mario Pederneiras was a symbolist with a strong romantic streak. His greatest passion was his home city, Rio, and he wrote tender poems to its skies, streets, gardens, landscapes, and to some aspects of its urban life. Here is a piece of his poetry:

In autumntime light is like an eternal sunset
More tuned to quietness than to noise;
It shines
In such a sweet and calm way
That it seems to have been made
Only for the state of soul
Of a convalescent.

We encounter a very different kind of symbolism in the verses of Augusto dos Anjos, a man fascinated by science and saturated with the reading of the monistic philosophers. In his sonnet "The Lament of Things" he tells us how it is sad for him to listen to the seconds pass, beat by beat, successively, while he hears, in underground sounds, the earthly abandoned Energy weep. He explains to us that it is the pain of unused Power, the mournful chant of profound dynamos which, having strength enough to move millions of worlds, lie in a static condition of nothingness. It is the sigh of the still unprecise form—he adds—of transcendental things that do not come into reality. It is the light that could not become even a single gleam. It is, in brief, the formidable and subconscious cry of pain of nature which stopped weeping in the rudimentary state of desire.

An incorrigible punster and an amiable Bohemian, fat Emilio de Menezes paid also his tribute to symbolism—the same way he had prayed before in the Parnassian temple. But he was above all a clever satirist whose verses are true works of art, full of an irreverent wit.

While all these movements were going on in the realm of prose and poetry, what about the theater in Brazil? The curse of the gods, of which I told you in one of my previous chapters, still hangs ruinously over the Brazilian literary scene. Dramatic literature was scarce and very bad. Its only shining star—I mean its only playwright worthy of some notice—was Arthur Azevedo, a man with an especial gift for repartee—a kind of small-scale Bernard Shaw. He wrote short stories and plays in humorous vein, and many of his wisecracks, puns, and sayings were famous at his time.

In the field of criticism there reigned two clumsy giants: Sylvio Romero and José Veríssimo. They were both industrious, honest, and boring. The former is the author of a monumental "History of Brazilian Literature" in five thick volumes. It is a remarkable work from the standpoint of research and method, and of sheer quantity of information. But it is very badly written, and it is hard for any reader to go through those compact pages. As for Veríssimo, he was a schoolteacher who never lost the habit of correcting people's mistakes. As a critic he was well meaning, and generally well informed. But his writing had no charm, and his views lacked sociological perspective. Another essayist of note was Araripe Junior, the first Brazilian to write a book on Ibsen.

Capistrano de Abreu is one of the most remarkable historians of the period and, like Varnhagen, he was hardworking, accurate, and without appeal to the common reader. His books are a thesaurus of information, rather than of ideas or of enlightening comments.

But in the intellectual arena of Brazil one figure loomed toweringly—at least in the mental sense, because it happened to be that of a short and lean little man with an enormous skull and a bristling mustache. His name? Ruy Barbosa. He was a lawyer, journalist, and speaker. Not only was he a powerful orator and an amazingly learned person; he was also perhaps the greatest authority on the Portuguese language in Brazil, and the man who used it with most effectiveness, beauty, and richness. His reputation was little by little becoming a legend. "What do you want to be when you grow up?" fathers and mothers asked their little sons. And the precocious creatures answered without winking: "A Ruy Barbosa!"

Between 1898 and 1899 the historical La Hague conference for universal peace was held and Ruy Barbosa played in it an important role as the representative of his country. Legend says that everybody was amazed to see that little swarthy fellow who could not only speak but also be eloquent in ten different languages. Returning victoriously from the conference, Ruy Barbosa received in his country the title of the "eagle of The Hague."

It is said that when he lived in London he had permanently pasted on the door of his flat a card with these words: "Dr. Ruy Barbosa, Teacher of English."

In London, of all places!

VII

The Century Was Young and Cynical

THE twentieth century entered rather gaily, full of scientific and philosophical promises. The detached cynicism which pervaded the atmosphere at the end of the previous century invaded the new one. In the Brazilian literary world you no longer found writers gathered in schools. Now you saw individuals, free lances, each of them with his peculiar traits and trends. Of course there were survivors, and very distinguished ones, of the literary currents of the nineteenth century. (I must add that Alberto de Oliveira, the high priest of the Parnassian poetry, died only a few years ago.) But the predominant note was disillusion and a kind of snobbish cynicism. The influence of the Portuguese novelist Eça de Queiroz was very clear on many of the Brazilian writers. But that of Oscar Wilde, the Goncourts, Anatole France, and d'Annunzio was no less conspicuous.

João do Rio is the pen name of Paulo Barreto, a columnist and storyteller who translated Wilde's "Salomé" and "The Portrait of Dorian Gray" into Portuguese. He wrote charming pages on Rio—its manners, religions, and people. He was sophisticated and, like Wilde, he believed that "life imitates art" rather than that art imitates life. In one of his tales—which he very cautiously places in a hypothetical country—he tells us about a young man who was honest, hardworking, and sensible but who, notwithstanding all that, could not succeed in life. One day he decided to see a watchmaker to ask him what was wrong with his head.

"Well," the watchmaker told him, "leave your head here. I want to examine its mechanism."

"But how can I go on living without a head?" asked the lad.

"That's easy," replied the other. "I shall give you a provisional cardboard head. Of course it is empty, but I think it will be all right for the time being."

"Okay," agreed the young man. "Here is my head."

And so the exchange of heads was made, and the hero of the tale started his life with his vacant cardboard head. From that moment on he did all sorts of foolish and unreasonable things, but surprisingly enough he succeeded well; he made a career and he became rich and famous. He was so happy that he forgot all about his real head. One day, passing by the watchmaker's shop, he entered and, out of pure curiosity, asked about his head.

"Well," said the man, "I found nothing wrong with your head, young man. It has the most amazingly precise mechanism I have ever seen in all my life. Congratulations!"

But the young man shook his head, smiling, and said: "No, good man. Keep it for yourself. I am very happy with my cardboard one. Good-by!"

Such a cynical story is intended to be a criticism of Brazilian society. And that reminds me of another tale, by Lima Barreto—a very interesting novelist also concerned with Rio de Janeiro, chiefly with its suburban life.

It is about a man who tells a friend, at a café table, how he achieved fame and made a career. Once, being jobless, he read in the paper an advertisement in which a family asked for a man who knew the Javanese language, to read for them an old book which was supposed to have a magical lucky influence on those who could listen to the reading of its contents. The man had an idea. He knew not a word of Javanese; but he consulted an encyclopedia, learned a few things about Java, its costumes, and some features of its language, and he applied for the job. Being hired, one night he took the sacred book and started giving its pages an imaginary translation. The family was very happy and paid him well, and his fame and authority in the Javanese language spread, and he was asked to write articles for philological reviews—which he did. In a short time he had a reputation, he had obtained other good jobs, and he was even appointed to represent Brazil at a European congress of the Javanese language.

The friend listened intently to the story, and when the other finished he said: "Do you know what I have decided to be from now on?"

"No."

"A prominent bacteriologist!"

Shifting between the sublime and the ridiculous was a really queer bird in the Brazilian literary fauna. It was Mucio Teixeira—to whom the emperor had given the title of Baron of Ergonte—a combination of playwright, poet, prophet, and soothsayer, with a passion for the occult.

Eduardo Prado, a wealthy *paulista*, a blasé globe-trotter, and a man of wit, libeled the United States in his book "The American Illusion," the first edition of which was confiscated by the Brazilian government in 1895. But Luiz Guimarães Filho, a poet and a diplomat, lovingly described Japan in "Samurais and Mandarins."

A diplomat, a politician, and a writer, Assiz Brasil was one of the most learned men of his times.

Grammatically impeccable, but rather bloodless and impassive in his writings, was the classical-minded Carlos de Laet. A touch of classicism we find also in poet and novelist Mario de Alencar, although his books have much more charm than Laet's. A man also in love with classicism was quaint José Albano, who wrote poems to Camões and to the Portuguese language.

Martim Francisco, a fine prosist, loved polemics, and his writings were a mixture of irony, pessimism, and epigrammatic humor.

A teacher, a critic, and a poet, Osorio Duque-Estrada is the author of the lyric of the Brazilian national anthem. A versatile and hard-working writer was Almachio Diniz.

Alfredo Pujol wrote a very substantial essay on his famous friend Machado de Assiz.

A distinguished diplomat and essayist, Joaquim Nabuco told of his education in an autobiographical book and expressed his views on life, men, and ideas in a book written in French: "Pensées Détachées."

One of the most beloved books of the first decade of the twentieth century was Felício Terra's heroic and sentimental stories on the war between Russia and Japan.

Prominent among the sociologists of the period was charmless, compact Oliveira Lima.

The best essays on the Brazilian Negro were those by Nina Rodrigues.

Many other writers were making their appearance on the scene, but only in the twenties did some of them attain any fame.

When the *bandeirantes* entered the northern backlands, in search of gold and precious stones, they left there, scattered over the wilderness, many descendants of theirs in small villages or on very rudimentary farms. They were generally mestizos and there they stayed like forgotten islands amid the vast *sertão*. The government never cared about them. They were far from the populous seaboard; they had no medical attention, no schools, no support of any kind. They led a rather barbaric life, and constituted dangerous sources of fanaticism and crime.

During the last decade of the nineteenth century a group of poor and ignorant folks gathered in the backlands of Brazil around a man known as "Antonio the Counselor," who was said to work miracles. They were illiterate, undernourished, and weather-beaten people with a natural craving for a happier life. Their primitive and superstitious souls, which longed eagerly for the supernatural, found in that bearded and rough prophet a father; a Messiah; a source of advice, hope, and joy. They founded a village, Canudos, that in a short while had about fifty-two hundred wood and mud huts which spread up and down the hills and throughout the valley. Its lanes, dead ends, and irregular streets were disorderly, disconcerting, and tortuous, like the very souls of its inhabitants. It is only natural that such a gathering of fanatical people meant trouble. The "Counselor" had chosen a dangerous catchword for his sermons: "Down with the republic!" His followers repeated that phrase in a hysterical frenzy. The population of Canudos was increasing tremendously. The whole *sertão* was infected with the legend of the "saint" whose citadel offered a safe haven for criminals and fugitives from justice. The "Counselor's" men started highway robbery; they also plundered ranches and villages to get money and materials to build their temples. In his long and dark tunic the somber "Prophet of the Backlands" announced the end of the world and promised his mob a better life in heaven, teaching them at the same time contempt for this wicked earthly existence.

One day the neighboring town of Joazeiro, which had sold a certain quantity of lumber for the "Counselor" to build his church, refused delivery. The "saint," affronted, sent his armed men to collect it. The Justice of Joazeiro telegraphed for protection. A force of about a hundred police was sent by train—only to meet with a crushing defeat. And in the following years that which seemed to be a simple *caso de polícia* turned into a real war. Federal troops, fully equipped with rifles and cannons, were sent to fight the rebels, and after many unsuccessful expeditions, and at the cost of heavy casualties, they managed at last to overcome the barbaric citadel. But "Canudos never surrendered. The only case of its kind in history, it held out to the last man. Conquered inch by inch, in the literal meaning of the words, it fell on October 5, toward dusk—when its last defenders fell, dying, every man of them. There were only four left: an old man, two other full-grown men, and a child, facing a furiously raging army of five thousand soldiers."

While that sinister drama was being staged in the backlands, the Brazilian literati, with very few exceptions, showed a supreme unconcern toward national problems. Some of them were still childishly in love with the mother tongue and kept playing with words, in the shadow of Ruy Barbosa—the man who, they proudly stated, had discovered in Portuguese forty synonyms for "prostitute." There were others who tried to imitate Flaubert, Zola, or the Goncourts. Europe was their meat, France their spiritual country, and Paris their favorite city.

Meanwhile Brazil was full of serious and provoking unsolved problems that nobody dared or cared to tackle. Politicians as usual were too much absorbed in politics. The republic was living its first troubled years; and the care of a new-born baby, you know, is always a delicate matter, especially for inexperienced parents.

Things were like that when, toward the close of the year 1902, Euclides da Cunha published his book "Os Sertões," which contained a very serious and profound study of the hinterland—its fauna, flora, geography, climate, geology, and ethnology—together with an unusually honest and

vigorous report on the campaign of Canudos. The book was
the work of an artist as well as of a scientist. It sounded like a
tremendous libel, and it had the effect of a bright and
ponderous meteor falling unexpectedly from the sky. Its
thud stunned for a moment critics, politicians, military men,
artists, literati, and common readers. Who was—they asked
—that brave man who dared to challenge the government,
making a crude and strikingly sincere report on a campaign
that some newspapers had tried to depict with noble and
glorious colors? Moreover, the astounding fellow had ended
his book with a two-line chapter which ran like this: "The
trouble is that we do not have a Maudsley for acts of madness
and crime on the part of nations."

Thousands of people were reading "Os Sertões." The
majority of the readers were fascinated chiefly by the style
of the writer. Many of them skipped the first two chapters—
"The Backlands" and "The Man"—because they found
them too overloaded with technical terms, but stayed
eagerly with the last part of the work—"The Rebellion"—
because it had the flavor of a good novel, full of plots, pathos,
and drama.

Da Cunha has a masculine style. His phrases are bright and
flexible like steel. They sparkle and sometimes they have the
lashing quality of a whip. His prose is often nervous, im-
patient, almost wild, but sometimes it gains a disciplined and
even cool tranquillity. But it is always precise and correct.
And the mathematician that Euclides da Cunha was makes
himself visible in the geometric quality of the sentences, in
the love of accuracy, and in the structure of the paragraphs.
Several passages of "Os Sertões" are really unmatched
masterpieces of Portuguese prose. In short, that book was an
important landmark; it inaugurated a new era in Brazilian
literature. Many of the literati who had their eyes turned
toward Europe and who were concerned merely with

aesthetic problems left their ivory towers and stepped down to the good old earth—following the trail of Euclides da Cunha, that nervous and rather timid little man who once had described himself in verse as a "mixture of Indian, Celt, and Greek." And after the publication of "Os Sertões" there sprang up throughout Brazil, with the luxuriance of tropical flora, a regional kind of literature whose heroes were country folks and whose landscapes were native, as native were, too, their problems, conflicts, and passions.

If I had to choose just one book in Brazilian literature to be translated into other languages as representative of my country and of my people, I would certainly pick "Os Sertões." It is really our greatest classic. It gives you the main key to the Brazilian soul. It is beautiful, clear-minded, and truthful. It is courageous, unbiased, and dramatic. It tells you about an amazing racial melting pot. It shows you, with an almost photographic likeness, a tragic landscape, both geographic and human. It narrates an impressive story of violence, fanaticism, blood, and misery, but a story, too, of indomitable courage and endurance. It is full of sympathy and pity for the underdog. And it is a book surprisingly "new" and timely, because many of the problems it presents and discusses are still to be solved.

Afonso Arinos in Minas Gerais had, a few years before, turned his eyes to the *sertanejo*, the man of the hinterland, writing a very charming book of short stories, "Pelo Sertão," many of whose pages you find today in almost all Brazilian anthologies.

Coelho Netto, a man frantically in love with words, a true dictionary worm, wrote also a book of *contos* named "Sertão," whose characters are simple folks who live near Mother Earth. But his enthusiasm for the regional literature did not last long. Soon he was interested again in city life and sophisticated problems, and he wrote about them many books in which there are really beautiful passages but which generally are ruined by sheer verbosity.

The drama of drought in the Brazilian northeastern region was powerfully described by Domingos Olympio in a rude novel, "Luzia Homem."

In the southernmost Brazilian state, Rio Grande do Sul, two writers portrayed the Gaucho and his wild life: Alcides Maya and Simões Lopes Netto. The former was academic, a bit gongoristic, and too word-conscious. The latter was truer to the countryfolk and life, having a kind of elemental strength. His short stories and legends have a sort of unsophisticated beauty.

Later on, in São Paulo, Waldomiro Silveira and Monteiro Lobato wrote charming stories on the hillbillies and their simple life. Their tales are not as grim as those of the northern part of the country, because São Paulo's hinterland is more populous and not so poor and forsaken as the Brazilian Nordeste.

There appeared at the beginning of this century another outstanding book: "Chanaan," by Graça Aranha. It may be considered the precursor of the novel of ideas in my country. It is masterfully written and constructed. Through Milkau and Lentz, two of its chief characters, the reader is confronted with the bewilderment of two cultured Europeans before the turmoil of Brazilian life and landscape. They talk, and they compare, and they wonder, and they discuss the future. Nature—the exuberant Brazilian nature—must be considered, too, a character in that novel.

A sociologist in love with his country and his people, Alberto Torres envisaged the national problems with a realistic eye.

And so, in the beginning of this agitated century of ours, there arose in Brazil a regional kind of literature provoked by Euclides da Cunha's masterpiece "Os Sertões." Their followers no longer saw the Indians and the mestizos as ideal fiction characters who spoke like academicians. They were no longer entranced before the beauties of the native landscape. They went on seeing gorgeous twilights, trees and lakes and flowers, but they also had eyes for the floods or the droughts. But if you analyze the work of many of those regionalists you will arrive at the conclusion that they did not envisage the whole thing in terms of a real human understanding. They did recognize the existence of social problems, but they never thought they had to be solved. The underdog was for many of them merely a subject.

When the first World War broke out in 1914, the Brazilian writers immediately took sides. They were pro-Allied. France was their spiritual fatherland. They made verses and wrote prose pages against the "barbarism of the Huns." In 1917 Brazil declared war on Germany. In 1918 there came the armistice. The forces of evil—they chanted —had been defeated. The Allies had made the world free for democracy. But had they really?

The Bolsheviks had overthrown the Russian empire. Anti-communist propaganda was started all over the world. There was a revolution going on in Germany.

Pale tired-looking men emerged from the trenches. War had made them old in their twenties or thirties. Some of them started writing books on their ghastly experiences. They were shocking books, because they did not speak the golden language of victory and heroism. They talked about lice, mud, blood, misery, death, and physical and moral deterioration. In Brazil the writers had "suffered" the war only through the news and the illustrated magazines. Few of them guessed that the world had become a very narrow corner, and that the most agitated years of Brazilian history and literature were yet to come.

VIII

The Eventful Twenties

LET us suppose you are in an airplane, flying high over an island. You look down and you can see the island in its entirety, with a definite shape, a clear-cut contour. You see it as a whole, without grasping its details. But if your plane loses altitude and gets nearer the island, you lose your general view, because the island widens, and you perceive that the design of its shores is not so neat or simple; that its outline is not made of long graceful curves, having on the contrary a rather complicated pattern which takes the form of inlets, capes, bays, lagoons, and so forth. Even the color of the island territory changes from a bluish green expanse, with some darker or brighter spots, to a true kaleidoscopic field in which you discover unsuspected colors and designs.

The same thing happens when you are writing about the literature of a country. When you speak of the past centuries you have the point of view of the man in the plane looking down from a high altitude to the island. Time is your best ally and adviser: it has made its reliable choice. You grasp the essential traits of each period; you pick up the right authors and the right books—in brief, you have a fair general outlook. But when you try to study the literature of your own day you lack a good perspective in time, because you are too close to your subject. Such a proximity is very dangerous, because out of a craving for precision and justice you pay a minute attention to the fanciful pattern of the island's contours, giving them an importance that mostly they really do not deserve.

I propose to write in the following chapters about these last twenty years or so of Brazilian literature. The whole thing is very difficult not only because my plane has lost most of its altitude but because, as a matter of fact, I am now within the island, as one of its inhabitants. I belong with it. I have there my friends and my foes; my favorite resorts, landscapes, forests, gardens, and skies, as well as many spots which I abominate or am indifferent to. That is the reason why sometimes I feel rather lost in that territory. My compass is too personally biased. And after all there are so many roads. . . .

Anyway I will gladly take all risks, and I invite the reader to join me for a short walk across the island's woods. I must tell you that it is not a civilized and charming forest like that European one which Beethoven so masterfully describes in his Pastoral Symphony. No, it is rather a jungle without order and sometimes without pity—an entangled jungle full of ridiculous monkeys as well as of gorgeous colorful birds; a dwelling place of bloody beasts and of innocent doves. We shall find there unhealthy dangerous swamps, full of mosquitoes, not far from placid clean lakes of azure bordered with beautiful trees. It is a noisy place, sometimes too sunny and sometimes too dark. Bright-colored flowers alternate there with horrid-looking reptiles. Fairies and goblins not seldom dance together with giants and pygmies. And what is the meaning of such a mixed-up and incongruous world? Only God knows, and God generally keeps His own secrets. He never tells. Maybe sometimes He speaks metaphorically and we do not understand Him

Now, my friends, are you willing to come with me? Perhaps the whole thing is not so colorful and picturesque as I announced. You know, I am no historian, philosopher, or essayist. I am just a simple storyteller, and the storyteller is the man who is always exaggerating things and persons for the sake of his own story. Maybe our excursion is going to be a flop, as usually happens not only with travels but also with drugs, books, and motion pictures: the real thing never fulfills completely the promises of its flamboyant advertisements.

One day I wrote the story of prehistory in the form of a novel for juvenile readers. I had great fun in writing the book, but sometimes the novelist in me rebelled against scientific facts. When you write a story you try to direct, as a kind of minor god, all your characters, making them say and do what you think necessary for the development of the plot. But when I was writing that book on the antediluvian monsters and tried to make a neat classification of those "pets" according to the various geological ages, I was surprised to meet on the scene some survivors which belonged to the preceding period. "What are you doing here, Mr. Brontosaurus?" I asked. "Don't you know you should have vanished from the scenery many centuries ago?"

The same thing happens when I glance at the Brazilian literary scene of the postwar years. Most of the writers in my country behaved as if nothing had happened to Europe and the world. They lived in a world of moonshine. They went on fabricating academic sonnets with many Greek goddesses, acanthus leaves, and nymphs. They dealt with a dead beauty. Their verses had no blood, no flesh, no soul. The things they wrote about in prose or verse had nothing to do with passions, problems, and facts of real life. The sound of the cannons and the lament of the wounded had not reached their Olympian world. Those literati were demigods. Literature for them was a kind of religion with complicated secret rites and hermetic temples. The whole thing was so ridiculous that a Latin-American writer said that

Brazilian literature was nothing more than an eternal sonnet constantly amended for better or for worse.

What about the politico-social panorama of Brazil? The republican regime had found the country unified and endowed with railroads, schools, academies, industrial plants, and many other improvements. In the colonial times all the governing positions were in the hands of the Portuguese elite. When Brazil attained her independence the Portuguese were dispossessed of their posts and the Brazilian rural aristocracy started to rule the country. The second empire, however, decided to follow a centralizing policy aiming at the unification of the nation. Its leaders knew very well that each landowner was a prospective baron, with his own army and his lust for power. In a word, they were dangerous sources of separatism. So the emperor, under the influence of his advisers, did his best to weaken the landowners by gradually abolishing the large rural states. Such a policy coincided with the decline of the sugar cane plantations, determined by the appearance in the market of beet sugar and by the competition of foreign products. The centralizing policy was also much aided by the prosperity of the coffee plantations in the central state of São Paulo.

As a consequence Brazil started the urban phase of her life. People fled from the rural zones toward the cities, where the two ancient great divisions of national society—the rich landowners and holders of governing positions on the one side, and a rather amorphous mass of people on the other side—gave place to a clearer class discrimination, reinforcing the embryo bourgeoisie and originating a kind of urban elite which was to rule the country. That hegira to the seaboard was very ruinous for the country. Of course, thanks to it, we have today such big and important cities as Rio and São Paulo. But on the other hand, while the seaboard cities prospered, the hinterland villages progressed very slowly, remained stationary, or perished. We may say that the growing of Brazil was rather acromegalic.

Euclides da Cunha's masterpiece "Os Sertões" focused the dramatic problem of the neglected populations of the backlands. But, strangely enough, critics reviewed it in terms of pure literature, and politicians did not understand the meaning of the book or they did not read it at all.

But the republic was going on very well, thank you. At least apparently. As usual after the colonial times there had been a rush toward government offices. There were many political parties throughout the country. Bureaucracy had increased tremendously. There was no sound financial scheme, and Brazilians had taken too much to the letter that saying according to which Brazil was the land of the future. They had started getting loans from abroad at high interest, and they invested those funds badly and never knew how to repay them. What they all wanted—politicians, governors, etc.—was to remain in power, to gain prestige, and to lead a comfortable life. They had their godsons and protégés, and their prestige was estimated according to their capacity for distributing favors. Yes, they made sonorous speeches full of promises and big words. And the years passed, and each four years the nation had a new president. When *"Senhor Presidente"* was about to quit he nominated his own successor, in order that the grafting machine they had so cleverly built up should not stop functioning. That is to say, the same gang of big shots was to stay directly or indirectly in power, getting the best of positions and opportunities for doing good business as lawyers, entrepreneurs, deputies, senators, and so forth. Theoretically the country had a democratic regime, but elections were generally frauded and it was impossible for the opposition parties to win.

Three large states of the Union disputed among them-

selves the supremacy in the political scene: São Paulo, Rio
Grande do Sul, and Minas Gerais. The *paulistas* were rich
and enterprising; the mineiros were sly as politicians; the
Gauchos, tough guys. Some of the national leaders were
politicos out of pure love for politics; it gave them the same
thrilling emotion as did playing roulette or betting in horse
races. Too much preoccupied with the political game-win-
ning elections, making their own propaganda, enjoying life,
distributing positions and favors, to gain voters and eventual
bodyguards, Brazilian leaders had no time to come to grips
with the really important problems of the nation.

We used to say that Brazil was so vigorous a country that,
no matter what the politicos did all the day long to ruin her,
she recovered naturally during the night. Brazilian people
have a fine sense of humor, a keen eye for the comical, and a
certain tendency toward pessimism. They watched their
politicians at play. Sometimes they followed them in many
campaigns, lured by promises of serious reforms in the political world. Not seldom Brazilians took part in revolutions, fighting for the ideals expressed through the speeches
of their leaders. But soon they were again disillusioned, because those very idealistic politicians whom they had raised
to power at the price of their sweat, blood, and tears proved
to be as selfish, greedy, and unreliable as the old ones. And
so indifference and apathy—those poisons which very easily
enter the blood of the Brazilians—tend to be the natural
state of mind of my people. Indifferent and apathetic they
were during the ten years which followed the end of the
first World War.

The attitude of the intellectuals was one of pessimism. The
old generation professed a nineteenth century cynicism. As
a matter of fact, they *were* still in the nineteenth century.
The middle generation assumed a very curious attitude: they
seemed to hint, under the influence of certain European

writers, that they belonged to the "lost generation of the trenches." But what trenches? They had taken part in the war only through the newspapers. But they knew that old taboos had been destroyed, that something new was about to arise. They were restless. They believed no more in sonnets, in ancient Greek symbols, and in old-fashioned formulas. They were already writing and speaking, many of them, about the new world. But they did not know what shape things and ideas were to take in that fresh universe.

Let us leave them in that uneasy situation and meet a short dapper fellow with a tanned bony face, thick black eyebrows, and dark sparkling eyes. His name is José Bento Monteiro Lobato. At that time he was almost thirty years old and completely unknown to the literary world. As a matter of fact, he was a lawyer; but he hated that profession. He lived in the country where he had a coffee plantation, in the state of São Paulo. He was worried because there was a tremendous drought in the land and, worse than that, huge fires had been lately devouring the dry woods in the neighborhood. The flames lasted about two months and people were really alarmed. Monteiro Lobato was so impressed with the fact that he wrote a long essay, in the form of an unpretentious letter, to the editor of the most important newspaper of São Paulo, giving his opinion as to the real cause of those fires. The editor read the letter and was so surprised to read such a beautiful and humorous piece of prose that he not only published it in his newspaper but also asked the author to send him more articles.

So Monteiro Lobato was transformed overnight into a man of letters. "I did not know that my letter was that good," he told me once. And the very subject of that letter gave him an idea for an essay which became famous, "Urupês." It is the portrait of the Brazilian hillbilly, drawn through the fictitious character named Jeca Tatú (Joe Armadillo). Jeca Tatú was hailed as a symbol, and a grim symbol at that. People laughed at his antics and sayings, but Jeca Tatú in reality was the light and humorous counterpart of those tragic fanatics whom Euclides da Cunha had described in his great book.

According to his creator, Jeca Tatú is impenetrable to progress and evolution. He is always squatting on his own heels, lazily smoking his clay pipe. When Dom Pedro I cried out "Independence or Death!" and Brazil attained her independence, Jeca stood up for a while, shot a casual glance at the scene, and squatted back again. When abolition came the Negro slaves threw away their hoes with an exclamation of relief, and got away. . . . Joe Armadillo scratched his head and waited for the coming of the European immigrant to replace the Negroes, as plantation workers. On November 15, 1889, a general told the people that the republic was proclaimed, but Jeca did not hear him. There was a revolution four years later, and some Brazilian men-of-war shelled Rio. But Joe was still squatting idly in the sun, ignoring the whole thing. He hated work. He used to sell in the next village market the things that grew wild about his neglected farm, the fruits and plants he could pick up easily without abandoning his squatting position. His house was of the most primitive and shabby kind, dilapidated and unlivable. Its walls were falling to pieces and its roof leaked badly, and when someone asked Jeca why he did not mend them the amazing creature answered simply: "Oh . . . it does not pay." When election day came he put on his best suit (which happened to be a very poor one) and went to town to vote. "For whom did you vote, Joe?" his wife asked him. Jeca made a grimace, lit his pipe, and answered: "Oh . . . I don't know. I voted for the government. That's all." And there he was again in his squatting position, with half-closed eyes, motionless like a fakir.

Monteiro Lobato concluded his essay with the following words: "Poor Jeca Tatú! You are so handsome in the novels and so ugly in real life! You don't talk; you don't sing; you don't love. And amid so much life only you don't really live."

The book in which such a pessimistic page was included had a very good sale all over the nation, but the figure of Jeca Tatú attained national fame only when Ruy Barbosa, the great orator and scholar of legendary reputation, quoted it in one of his famous speeches. However, Monteiro Lobato tried to prove that Jeca Tatú was lazy and apathetic just because the government did not pay any attention to him. Joe was illiterate; he had no medical attention—he lived as an outcast.

Monteiro Lobato abandoned rural life, moved to São Paulo, and started his literary career. He was no dreamer. He had a practical mind. He was enterprising and clearminded. He founded a literary magazine, "Revista do Brasil," and a publishing house which inaugurated a new era in the publishing business in Brazil, which hitherto had followed the French conservative methods as regards book covers and advertisements. Many writers gathered around Monteiro Lobato. Later on, some of them won repute. Such is the case of Leo Vaz, a quiet unassuming newspaperman, who wrote "Professor Jeremy," the story of a provincial schoolteacher. It is an excellent psychological novel very much in the Machado de Assiz vein. Another of the many writers launched by Lobato was Gastão Cruls, a man with Dutch blood in his veins and a son of a distinguished astronomer. He wrote an interesting book of short stories on regional subjects.

The great best-seller of the time was Menotti del Picchia's "Juca Mulato," a romantic love story told in verse with pleasant rhymes and images. It took the country by storm, and was followed by two other successful poems by the same author: "Masks" and "Don Juan's Sorrow." "Idle Life," by Godofredo Rangel, a close friend of Lobato, was hailed by critics as a masterpiece of its kind. Rosalina Coelho Lisboa arose as a kind of imposing priestess of the Parnassian credo with her "Pagan Rite," a collection of well-made sonnets.

Lobato went on writing. He had much of the humorist, and not seldom his humor was tinged with sarcasm. He was outspoken and incisive. He scorned the politicians and he never trusted them. Nevertheless, he always refrained from writing propaganda books. When he wanted to criticize men and things Brazilian, he summoned his fictitious character, Mr. Slang, an Englishman, and let the queer old fellow talk in his quiet and ironical way. I like Lobato as a writer and as a man. Some of his tales are simple anecdotes; but even when they lack a deeper meaning, they are always highly readable and clever. Lobato's short stories "The Patchwork Quilt," "The Little Negro Girl," and "The Lighthouse Keepers" are undoubtedly among the best pages ever written in the Portuguese language.

Outside Lobato's circle there were various outstanding poets and prose writers.

Everything indicated that a new "geological era" was beginning for Brazilian literature. As a magnificent representative of the big reptilian age there was still Alberto de Oliveira, writing his clever but stiff, stony sonnets with the patience of a crossword puzzle addict. But there were some changes in the appearance of the new Parnassian poets. Let us take, for instance, Raul de Leoni, a young man with Italian blood. He was much more human than most of the Brazilian Parnassians. His voice was clear and bright, and the best definition of the quality of his poetry is the very title of his book: "Mediterranean Light." In one of his beautiful sonnets he gives the reader the following advice.

> *Love the unuseful things! Dream. . . . As to life,*
> *Well, you have seen that life is but a vague appearance*
> *And all the immense dream that you scatter*
> *Is but a distracted golden legend*
> *That the ironic waves read and wipe*
> *Out of the voluble memory of the sands.*

Da Costa e Silva's "Zodiac" is a remarkable book of poems in which we find something quite new concerning rhythm and images. And Ronald de Carvalho's "Poems and Sonnets" revealed an aesthetician and a real poet in love with Parnassus as well as with Omar Khayyám and Anacreon. Gilka Machado wrote fine erotic poems which shocked many readers, who avoided looking at her book "The Naked Woman" as if each copy of it were indeed a nude woman.

Another poet of note is Olegario Marianno, who chanted the cicadas. A romantic at heart, he has none of the rigidity of many Parnassians. In his "Running Water" and "The Last Cicadas" you find beautiful poems which are still very popular throughout Brazil.

One of the most gifted poets of his or any other generation is Guilherme de Almeida, whose "Messidor" was a national best-seller. Clever, sensitive, always a man of good taste and many literary resources, he made quite a reputation with half a dozen works, among which is a noteworthy translation of François Villon's ballads.

In the field of fiction there were, to begin with, Julia Lopes de Almeida's novels on city life and problems, in the naturalistic tradition. And Xavier Marques, a romantic realist, wrote stories whose background was Bahia and whose characters were generally its fishermen and countryfolk; his "Jana and Joel" is a moving love tale.

Afranio Peixoto is a distinguished scholar who has written with great skill on many subjects. His first novel, "The Sphinx," is a fine psychological story about an enigmatical woman. In his later novels—"Maria Bonita" and "Wild Fruit"—the author abandoned the urban setting to write about people and life in the country, but all his heroines have still a touch of sophistication.

Another amazingly versatile writer was the always readable Medeiros e Albuquerque, who wrote about practically everything—from fiction to politics, from grammar to hypnotism. His frank memoirs were published posthumously under the title of "When I Was Alive."

João Ribeiro was another scholar of note. Congenial and understanding, still a young man in his seventies, he was an undisputed authority in the fields of philology, history, literature, art, sociology, and folklore.

An amazing character was worldly José do Patrocinio Filho, a combination of Baron Munchausen and Oscar Wilde. A fascinating *causeur*, he did not live; he acted. He was Bohemian, congenial, versatile, unreliable, and charming. He boasted of being an intimate friend of many European celebrities, artists, writers, actors, and even kings. He lived like a prince and died like a pauper.

One of the most important novelists of the period was Bohemian Lima Barreto, who followed the literary tradition of Manuel Antonio de Almeida and Machado de Assiz. In his very interesting novels he depicted the suburban life of Rio.

The life story of Humberto de Campos is really impressive. Born in poverty in one of the northern states of Brazil, he had, like Charles Dickens, a difficult and laborious childhood and adolescence. Through his newspaper work in Rio he made a reputation for himself, first as a columnist and later as a poet, and became a member of the Brazilian Academy of Letters. During the last years of his eventful life he suffered from a horrible disease—a brain tumor—which deprived him of his sight. Nevertheless he went on writing his daily syndicated column, and that was perhaps the most prolific period of his life. Thousands of persons looked eagerly for Humberto de Campos' column. News of the writer's illness had spread throughout the country and lent poignancy to his writings, which were surprisingly clear, fluent, and beautiful. When Humberto de Campos' "Memoirs" were published, Brazil saw in it one of her greatest bestsellers. So great was the demand for his works that his publishers brought out new editions of all his former books, the sale of which was enormous. After a painful agony Humberto de Campos died, a famous man on the verge of becoming rich. But fame and fortune had come too late, and at too great a cost.

In the field of the historical novel the most successful of all Brazilian authors was Paulo Setubal, who wrote "The Marchioness of Santos" (a story about the mistress of Pedro I, first emperor of Brazil), "The Prince of Nassau," and many other works. A few years before his death Paulo Setubal was converted to Catholicism, and wrote a very moving book on his conversion: "Confiteor."

Alberto Rangel, evidently under the spell of Euclides da Cunha's style, described the Amazon jungle in his "Green Hell."

Philosophical problems were tackled very competently by Farias Brito in "The Physical Basis of the Mind." Vicente Licinio Cardoso, a remarkably learned person, is the author of "The Philosophy of Art." And cultured Pontes de Miranda, one of the most authoritative jurists of the country (it is said that Ruy Barbosa launched him by praising a work of his, when he was still in his twenties), wrote skillfully on the subject that was his speciality, and on philosophy.

A man of many talents is Gilberto Amado, a brilliant poet and prosist.

Tristão de Atahyde (pen name of Alceu de Amoroso Lima) wrote a fine biography of the author Afonso Arinos. Serious-minded Jackson de Figueiredo went on in his quest of God and truth in "Pascal and Modern Inquietude."

Brazil was always rich in irreverent columnists like Antonio Torres, a man who had a feud with the Portuguese in general and with the members of the Brazilian Academy of Letters in particular. His prose was correct, fluent, rich, and spiced with a delightful sense of humor. Paulo da Silveira followed the same line in his "Wings and Paws." Another bold and irreverent writer is cultured, clever Gondin da Fonseca—whose translation of Wilde's "Ballad of Reading Gaol" is a work of art.

Agrippino Grieco, a man with Italian blood in his veins, is a writer with a keen eye for the grotesque and a talent for repartee. His victims are the stuffed-shirts, the conspicuous bourgeois, and the pompous academicians. He loves to devastate the work of his fellow authors. If by any chance he had to praise someone, the result would be a poor and colorless page. His style has a kind of permanent high pitch, just like his voice. His face has the profile of a Punch. He is caustic and nothing is sacred for him. Some of his enemies say that he is so venomous that if he happened to bite his own tongue he would be poisoned to death. I find him tremendously clever, and his prose style to my taste is vivid, colorful, and witty. Demolition is his speciality, but for demolishing reputations and taboos he never uses high explosives. No, that would be in bad taste; and Grieco, after all, has a Renaissance mind. He uses, instead, poison, a poniard, and fireworks. And when the whole building is reduced to ruins, there he is—the demolisher—among the debris, laughing like a mad Punch.

IX

The Stone and the Road

IT WAS still in the eventful twenties—to be precise in 1922—
that some writers and artists in São Paulo held the famous
meetings known in the annals of Brazilian literature as "The
Week of Modern Art." A group of men—poets, prosists,
painters, and musicians—influenced, if I am not mistaken,
by Marinetti, Blaise Cendrars, and Jean Cocteau, and irritated by the impassibility of the academicians and the in-
eptitude of the big shots of the art world, decided to lay
the basis of a new art more expressive of their country and
their time. They declared: "Down with all literary taboos!
We are living in a new age of dynamic forces! This is the
century of the airplane and of the radio! Down with the
Olympic gods! Down with the sonnet! Down with the conventional means of artistic expression! Down with grammar! Down with silly rhyme and enslaving meter! Let us
make free verse that is dynamic and full of bold images cast
in new molds! Down with melancholy! We are the children
of a new and rich land, and we must be joyful and strong!
Let us write a literature that is truly Brazilian, one that smells
of our earth and represents more truthfully the dreams of
our people!"

Among the leaders of the new revolutionary movement
were Mario de Andrade and Oswald de Andrade, both of
them *paulistas*. Here is an example of Mario de Andrade's
modern poetry from his book "The Hallucinated City."

LANDSCAPE NUMBER 3

Is it raining?
A grey drizzle smiles,
Very sadly, like a sadly long. . . .

The Emporium has not a clearance sale of raincoats
But here in this square
I may open my paradoxical umbrella,
This lyrical plane tree of sea laces. . . .

Across the street . . . "Mario, put on your mask!"
"You are right, my Madness, you are right."
The king of Thule has thrown his cup into the sea.

Men pass all soaked . . .
The reflections of their short figures
Taint the sidewalks. . . .
The doves of the Normal School building
Flutter among the fingers of the drizzle. . . .

(What if I include a Crisfal's poem
In the De Profundis? . . .)
All of a sudden
A coy sunbeam
Trespasses on the drizzle.

Oswald de Andrade is one of the brightest and most amusing characters I have met in my life. He is restless, imaginative, roguish, and bold. He was one of the most enthusiastic leaders of the "new school," and among the first who tried to give Brazilian poetry a national quality. One of his contributions to modernism was a book of poems called "Brazil Wood."

Carlos Drummond de Andrade, a clean-cut bespectacled young man born in the state of Minas Gerais, published his famous poem "In the Middle of the Road," which today is considered a kind of classic of the modern school. Here it is.

IN THE MIDDLE OF THE ROAD

In the middle of the road there was a stone
there was a stone in the middle of the road
there was a stone
in the middle of the road there was a stone.

I will never forget that event
in the life of my so very tired retina
I will never forget that in the middle of the road
there was a stone
there was a stone in the middle of the road
in the middle of the road there was a stone.

"But that young fellow is stark mad!" came from the opposing literary camp. "That so-called poem is pure schizophrenia!" The *modernistas* hurled back: "Schizophrenia my eye! That's a sound psychological poem. It is the drama of obsessing ideas."

And there lay the stone in the middle of the road. The modern writers decided to pick it up and throw it at the windows of the building that housed the Academy of Letters. The Brazilian literary scene became agitated and that agitation coincided with a revolution or, rather, with a riot, the forerunner of a series of military uprisings which were to occur periodically in Brazil.

The "futurists" or "modernists" acquired hundreds of proselytes. They published a manifesto. They were intoxicated with the idea of destruction. The initial phase of their movement was purely destructive. The *poetas modernos* wrote poems without meter or rhyme, with the visible intention of shocking formal writers and readers. Almost all of them were humoristic and rather obscure. Soon the Indianistic tendency was detected among the members of the new school. They planned to go back once again to Mother

Earth, but this time without the false lyricism of the romantic Indianists. And, as in most cases, their Indianism had a facetious trend; they published a manifesto in which they proclaimed themselves *antropófagos* (cannibals) who proposed to devour the forty academicians. What a banquet!

By this time the reader is certainly thinking that such a movement was too silly to deserve our further attention. But, if you think so, you are mistaken. Of course, there was a lot of tomfoolery about that idea of modernity. Hundreds of bad poets (if poets at all) appeared, lured by the facilities of the new school which had banned rhyme and meter. But the *modernistas* did a splendid work in rebelling against the conventional kind of literature we had in Brazil in those days, and in calling the attention of writers, poets, musicians, and painters to our own life, problems, and environment. When the period of destruction ended, writers and artists tried to build up something solid upon the ruins of the old school. Gone were the days of humorous repartee, liberties, and irreverences. The generation of the late twenties was no longer academic and conventional, but at the same time it had few vestiges of the early futuristic extremisms. The new poets and novelists had learned that language is only a means of expression and not an end in itself, and that true poetry does not depend solely on the pure beauty of words. Those first modernists had a sense of destiny, and in many ways they understood the age in which they were living. To explain better what they did, I must employ an image taken from the warfare of today. The pioneers of the modernistic movement in Brazil may be compared with that first wave of American marines which landed in Tarawa under heavy enemy machine-gun fire. Few of them escaped, but they had established a beachhead.

The first important adhesion—if I may use this word—to the new school was that of Manuel Bandeira, a poet of Parnassian leanings whom Mario de Andrade considers to be the "Saint John the Baptist of modernistic poetry." With his book "Dissolute Rhythm" he gave a priceless contribution to modernism.

Guilherme de Almeida, who had a brilliant record as a poet of the old school, joined the youthful crowd and, as he was a genuine poet, he succeeded in writing beautiful poems in accordance with the new patterns.

Many of the modern poets were so imbued with the love of their country that they started using the word *brasilidade* (Brazility) with a sickening obsession.

One of them, Cassiano Ricardo, wrote a book entitled "Let Us Go Hunting Parrots," the poems of which form a sort of wild canvas painted in bright lavish colors—full of golden spotted jaguars, green and yellow parrots, red tropical flowers, fanciful twilights, and lustrous green banana trees. Here is one of them.

LIGHTNING

The spotted jaguar climbed the tree trunk
in a lightninglike spring
Zut!
But an arrow, swifter than the lightning,
Made that matinal, electric, mustached big cat tumble on the
spot.
And there it remained like a colorful fruit fallen from a tree.

An important acquisition of modernism was Jorge de Lima, an astoundingly clever literary jack-of-all-trades, whose "Essa Nega Fulô," a folkloric poem, is undoubtedly one of the most remarkable specimens of Brazilian poetry.

In 1924 the *modernistas* acquired another very valuable proselyte. Graça Aranha, the author of "Chanaan," one of Brazil's great classics, during a meeting of the Academy of

Letters delivered a speech which threw the house into a panic. Notwithstanding his being a member of the "illustrious company," an aesthetician, a humanist, and a respectable man in his late fifties, Graça Aranha addressed his colleagues just to say they were a bunch of old men with fossilized minds; that their ideas and literary tastes and patterns were old-fashioned and worn out; and that they were incapable of grasping the real meaning of the moment mankind was living. He cried out that the world belonged to the young men, and that the *Academia* had to change its methods or die. The young modern writers who attended the session as guests applauded the lecturer madly, and carried him on their shoulders like a victorious prize fighter. The adherents of the "old school" did the same with Coelho Netto, the living symbol of "passadism."

With Ronald de Carvalho, who had belonged to the symbolist and Parnassian tradition, the modernists found one of their first balanced voices. He wrote "Ironical and Sentimental Epigrams," a book in which we detect an effort to make something out of modernism. Ronald de Carvalho was an aesthetician and a man in love with clarity. The following poem of his has the reticent gracefulness of a haikai.

CHAMBER MUSIC

A water drop slides on the windowpane,
A swallow darts swiftly through the air.
A lost leaf flutters,
  flutters. . . .
The rain falls slowly.

Evidently under the spell of Walt Whitman's poetry, Ronald de Carvalho later wrote his "The Whole of America," a colorful collection of pictures of the American continent.

Among the many adepts of modernism during the twenties, there were distinguished poets of Parnassian and symbolist tradition. Every one of them displayed different traits and leanings, as regards not only form but also ideas.

Raul Bopp was cosmic and folkloric. His "Cobra Norato" is an impressive poem of the Amazon jungle. This poet's language is very different from Ronald de Carvalho's. Listen.

The moon rose with rings around her eyes,
And silence hurts within the jungle.

The watching stars spy the night, from the outside. . . .

The shadow is eating slowly the swollen horizons.
This river is feverish
And the resigned waters march on, sinking in the soft
swamps. . . .

There are lone voices mumbling,
Tiny watery noises,
And a smell of torn carotides.
It seems that someone is coming, through the famished roots.

Ribeiro Couto is a lyric at heart, his voice having a hushed quality. Menotti del Picchia, on the contrary, is a painter in love with colors, whereas Tasso da Silveira is more concerned with the destiny of the human soul and with the mystery of life.

Sentimentality under the disguise of irony is what you find in most of the poems by Alvaro Moreyra, a poet who had paid his tribute to symbolism and who was to survive all the *isms*—to be, during the twenties, the thirties, and into the forties, just himself: a man apart, personal, restrained, clear-minded, master of a kind of prose for which I find no name because I think it is his own creation. His close friend, handsome athletic Felipe de Oliveira (he died in 1932, in Paris) was an unusual mixture of aesthetician, globe-trotter, a man in love with life and physical beauty and sports. A former symbolist, he turned modernistic in his book "The Green Lantern."

Once a symbolist, Murillo Araujo, author of sun-drenched poems full of exquisite images, needed only to take a short step forward to become a modernist—which he did very nicely in his book "The Illumination of Life."

But there was a feeling of unrest in the air, a feeling that something was going to happen. The modernist nucleus was about to split. The first years of the new school had in many ways been just a joyful play on words. Times had changed. The revolution of modern times was beginning to be felt in South America. Artists and writers were now conscious of their social responsibility. There were many serious and urgent problems, both material and moral, clamoring for solution. They felt they could no longer remain on the side lines of social debate and events.

People had begun to wonder what was really happening inside Russia. Many thought of Lenin's country with awe, others with fascination. But, communism or no communism, times were different and something quite dramatic and important was going to happen. Mussolini was trying to revive in Italy the fighting imperialist spirit of ancient Rome. There was chaos in Germany. The impact of European ideas on Brazil was immediate and strong. The airplane and the radio had made the world a very narrow corner. The great crisis of 1929 was approaching. In the midst of so many political and social issues, Brazilian writers felt they had to take sides. The republic in their country had failed. Brazil had tremendous natural resources still undeveloped. There were poverty, illiteracy, and bad health among the lower classes. The intellectuals felt that something had to be done. They were reading communist and fascist authors. They were looking to the left and to the right, in search of a solution, and not a few among them were looking upward, to heaven, to God. The academic writers generally were behaving rather like heavy, well-fed oxen in a continuous process of rumination. They ruminated upon their own glory and past achievements. They had attained immortality. They lived on Mount Olympus. But the young modernists had their feet on solid ground, now that their demolishing fury and their roguish pranks had become a thing of the past.

In my opinion the modernist movement was a kind of crossroads whence originated the multiple roads of the Brazilian literary scene of today. Of these various roads (some of them are just bypaths) I consider only three to be really important. One of them took the direction of the left with Oswald and Mario de Andrade, who were not communists but socialists who put a great emphasis on the importance of the economic factor in social life. The second road led to God, via the Vatican. The leader of the group which went neo-Catholic under the influence of such French writers as Péguy, Maritain, Claudel, etc., were Jackson de Figueiredo and Tristão de Atahyde. The leftists thought the crisis was chiefly economic; for neo-Catholics the whole thing was a question of lack of faith. As to the third road— it was a later prolongation of the second one toward the extreme right.

The leader of such a movement was Plinio Salgado, a novelist of note who had written one of the most important of the modernist books in the field of fiction: "The Foreigner." It is the story of some Italian immigrants who arrive poor in Brazil and, through hard work, thrift, and tenacity, grow rich while the traditional local family declines for lack of will and incentive. The whole book has a slight jingoist tang. Its characters are definitely symbolic and the moral of the story seemed to contain an invitation to patriots to react and take possession of the land of their ancestors.

In one 'of his subsequent novels, "The Expected One," Plinio Salgado drew the portrait of the Savior, the man who was about to come to save the country and lead it to a noble and glorious destiny. The closing words of the book are the following: "Brazil is on the march . . . crowds spring up on all sides. That is not the noise of the sea, nor of the forests, nor of the wind. I hear marching steps. . . . Whither?" Yes, whither? Plinio Salgado himself gave the answer, not only in words but in deeds. To fascism! And who was the expected one? Himself, of course. With the faith of an ancient prophet he started preaching his credo and founded the *Partido Integralista Brasileiro*, whose symbol was the sigma and whose partisans wore a green shirt and saluted like Mussolini's *camice nere* and Hitler's brown shirts.

Left, right, and center—these are the main roads which derived from that teeming and colorful crossroads which was the *movimento modernista*.

In 1924 Captain Luiz Carlos Prestes, a military engineer still under thirty, led a rebellion against the Brazilian government. He was a man with a wonderful record both as a student and as a soldier. Short, lean, swarthy, and taciturn, with a rather sad but serene face, he had not the appearance of what he really was; that is to say, a man of extraordinary intelligence and tremendous energy, a born leader. The nationwide scheme to overthrow the government failed, but Prestes went on. Having risen with a relatively small group of men in the town of Santo Angelo, in the southernmost state of Brazil, he refused to surrender and fought the numerous regular troops which were sent after him. Reports of his feats spread throughout the country, and many men left their families and their jobs to join the revolutionary column. That was the beginning of one of the most amazing legends of modern Brazilian history. Prestes and his men, always pursued by superior forces, made a fantastic march, on horseback, of more than five thousand miles, from Rio Grande do Sul to the northern state of Bahia. He was popularly known as the "Knight of Hope," and his exploits inspired many poems and pages of prose. The rebels climbed mountains, waded rivers, went through the jungles, fighting the enemy and the weather and at the same time arousing the feeling of rebellion among the villages, farms, and small towns of the Brazilian hinterland. And after a long strife, when victory became hopeless, the famous *coluna Prestes* was disbanded and its leader escaped into exile.

The whole thing had the virtue of instilling enthusiasm and hope of better times into the soul of the ordinarily apathetic Brazilian population.

In 1930 there was another popular revolution, backed by a large part of the army, which overthrew the government of Washington Luiz under the pretext that "it was not a democratic one, since the President, whose term was about to expire, had had the audacity to appoint his successor and have him elected through bribery, threats, and fraud."

Getulio Vargas was raised to power, as provisional President of Brazil, amid popular cheers. On October 24, 1930, there began what was to be called the "New Brazil." Invited to join the revolution, Luiz Carlos Prestes refused his collaboration because—he said frankly—he did not believe that a mere change of men could make things any better in the country, as long as he was convinced that the root of all evil was in the regime. In exile the "Knight of Hope" had read Soviet books, met communist agents. Now red was the color of his flag. And in exile he remained, because that was not the revolution of his dreams.

The thirties had started. Many political idols were shattered. New gods were rising. There was a fresh dewy smell of dawn in the air. People were full of hope and joy, because the newspapers said, everybody said, that a new era was beginning—an era of freedom, true democracy, and happiness. The October Revolution seemed to have put an end to corruption, disguised dictatorship, nepotism, and injustice.

New writers and artists were beginning to appear. Almost all of them were now socially conscious. Yes, on the Brazilian horizon there were unmistakable signs of a splendid aurora.

X

A Literature Comes of Age

IN THE thirties critics began to draw up the balance sheet of modernism. Of course there were profits and losses. None of them cared about the losses, but when they started estimating the profits they were unanimous in mentioning some poems by Ronald de Carvalho, Manuel Bandeira, Augusto Meyer ("Prayer for the Little Negro Shepherd"), Jorge de Lima ("Essa Nega Fulô"), and Raul Bopp ("Cobra Norato"). As to the field of prose—towering above a heap of literary junk they all saw a major book, Mario de Andrade's "Macunaíma," the "hero with no character at all," an Indian-blooded Brazilian who epitomizes some of the qualities and defects of his race. He is imaginative, restless, roguish, sensual, tricky, tender, and humorous. The book, a splendid allegory, is boldly and cleverly written in "Brazilian"; and by that I mean that Andrade used the language that is really spoken by the common people of Brazil, regardless of Camões and all the many generations of Portuguese and Brazilian classicists and grammarians. It is a curious lingo full of idiomatic expressions and picturesquely rich and flexible, colorful and informal. Macunaíma is a kind of Peer Gynt of the tropics. And the whole story, in its apparent disorder and formlessness, is a very valuable piece of folklore as well as an exquisite work of art.

The thirties brought to Brazilian literature its coming of age. The traits of adolescence—a taste for mere play on words and colors, the lack of the spirit of analysis—were vanishing. (Machado de Assiz in the previous century had been a kind of miracle in the field of fiction, and Euclides da Cunha a precursor in the realm of history and sociology.)

I may say that, after 1930, writers in my country started being interested in the social and philosophical problems of their times. The horizons of criticism widened. The majority of our novelists now write their stories around social problems. And those who think that economic factors are not capital take to the psychological novel. Anyway, they know that a novel is more than a clever plot or a series of events told gracefully only for entertainment purposes.

No doubt we had suffered all those previous years from a kind of "colonial complex," and out of a feeling of inferiority we were led to follow eagerly the European intellectual fashions. Our imitative urge meant in the last analysis that we were anxious to tell the world that we, too, "could do that"; that is to say, we, too, could write naturalistic novels like Zola's, symbolist poems like Mallarmé's, or shocking, crude novels like Marguerite's. Many of our men of letters used to write in French. Generally they refrained from depicting the life of our hillbillies, cowboys, and common folks, because in doing that they could not display their knowledge of Europe and its philosophers and artists. And nothing irritated them more than to be referred to by the French as *ces sauvages là-bas*, "those savages down there."

Who or, rather, what facts are responsible for our *cure?* The decline, if any, of French literature in the last twenty years? The trends of the postwar world? The economic crash of 1929? The many Brazilian revolutions? Or just . . . time? I think that all of those combined factors contributed to our almost complete cure. Yes, I think our literature has just come of age. And if you still detect in it some traces of immaturity—well, it is because even in old age we sometimes find vestiges of childhood.

Let us in this chapter cast a glance at the Brazilian literary scene of today in all fields but fiction.

The social problems of the northeast have been tackled very ably by Gilberto Freyre, who is perhaps the most distinguished of the living sociologists of Brazil. He writes informally, in a very colorful way, and one must say that he dispossessed sociology of its stiff shirt and frock coat—to make it wear light sporting clothes. You read his books with real gusto, as if they were highly entertaining novels. Another first-rate sociologist, Oliveira Vianna, is very much concerned with the racial problem in Brazil, and he has tried to prove that—the rate of mortality among the Negroes and Indians being high and the birth rate low, while the opposite is the case among the white population—in a not very remote future the population of Brazil will be almost completely white. Oliveira Vianna is the author of many books on sociology which are considered to be of the first rank.

Affonso Arinos de Mello Franco wrote an unusual book entitled "The Brazilian Indian and the French Revolution." His, too, is a clever essay on Brazilian civilization.

Outstanding among those who write about the Brazilian Negro is Arthur Ramos.

Sergio Buarque Hollanda is the author of a well-written essay, "The Roots of Brazil." Caio Prado Junior published the first volume of his monumental work "The Formation of Contemporary Brazil." Cassiano Ricardo gave up poetry to follow the road of social and political studies, writing "March to the West." "Rondonia," by the distinguished scholar Roquette Pinto, is considered a classic of modern times in its field.

Unassuming but very cultured Anizio Teixeira digressed on "Education for Democracy." Learned and understanding Angyone Costa writes competently on anthropology and archeology.

Azevedo Amaral described brilliantly in one of his books, "The Political Adventure of Brazil"; Paulo Prado painted a rather grim portrait of his country; and Octavio Faria made an impressive literary debut with his "Machiavel and Brazil."

Pedro Calmon wiped the dust from the textbooks of history, making them readable, thanks to his clear and pleasant style. Antonio de Alcantara Machado, an essayist of distinction, wrote a minor classic in "Life and Death of a Bandeirante."

In the field of biographical essays my favorites are Lucia Miguel Pereira's fine biography of Machado de Assiz, brilliant Vianna Moog's "Eça de Queiroz and the Nineteenth Century," and Edgar Cavalheiro's life of the romantic poet Fagundes Varella. Eloy Pontes, who is also a very sincere and outspoken book reviewer, wrote sound biographies of the Brazilian authors Raul Pompeia, Euclides da Cunha, and Machado de Assiz. Top-ranking among autobiographies are Rodrigo Octavio's "My Memoirs of Others," Oliveira Lima's recollections, and Graça Aranha's "The Romance of My Life."

Both a man of science and a distinguished man of letters is Miguel Ozorio de Almeida. A writer with no published book, but a great influence on many modern literati, Annibal Machado, amiable and scholarly, is a true poet even when writing in prose. One of the most significant figures of his generation, a learned man and a serious artist, Augusto Meyer does not care about being "popular"; clarity, balance, and restraint are the main qualities of his beautiful prose.

Psychological and philosophical problems are the meat of

such serious writers as Leonel Franca, Almir de Andrade, Hamilton Nogueira, and Bezerra de Freitas.

And here we meet again versatile Mario de Andrade as an important critic of art and literature, and the author of "Music, Sweet Music" and "The Ball of the Four Arts." Almiro Rolmes Barbosa collected in a book his charming essays on modern American authors.

Ronald de Carvalho's "Little History of Brazilian Literature" is a real masterpiece in its line. Nelson Werneck Sodré bares the economic foundations of Brazilian literature in a well-written book. Excellent are the literary "panoramas" by Afranio Peixoto. And another valuable work on the evolution of literature in Brazil is one in three volumes by Arthur Motta.

One of the most important literary critics in Brazil is undoubtedly Tristão de Atahyde. Unfortunately his strong Catholic leanings make him rather biased as a book reviewer. (His opponents call him the "Brazilian White Pope.") His contribution to Brazilian literature is really first-rate, and his prose is limpid and harmoniously precise.

Still in his early thirties, Álvaro Lins appears as one of the foremost critics of the country. He is serious-minded, erudite, and acute. I find in him only one defect, which belongs with the man but which sometimes spoils the writer. I mean his snobbishness, which leads him to disdain simple unpretentious writing. He hates so much the idea of being considered shallow or naïve that he feels unhappy whenever he is not able to quote in his reviews "profound" philosophers and writers. He usually scorns all the socially conscious writers who think it is possible to build a better world for the underdog. He calls them naïve utopians and, despite his sophistication, he seems to hint that there is no solution on this earth, the real happiness being only attainable in the next world—where the souls of those who behaved well in this vale of tears get an immaculate pair of wings, a snowy gown, a harp, and eternal life. . . .

In the state of Minas Gerais there is a brilliant group of essayists, and outstanding among them are Oscar Mendes and Eduardo Frieiro.

In the deep south Moisés Vellinho strikes me as being one of the most remarkably balanced of Brazilian critics. He has an accurate sense of values, good taste, and profundity; besides, he is a master as a prose stylist. In the same state another essayist of note, sensitive, learned, and deeply discerning—Carlos Dante de Moraes is the author of three very important books on men and ideas. And Manoelito de Ornellas, one of the first poets to rise in the south to the trumpet call of the modernists, is today among the most representative writers of the "Gaucho land"; his style is brilliant, colorful, and eloquent.

A fine ironist and a man endowed with an especial talent for generalizations is Vianna Moog, whose style, which sparkles with satire, has a particular appeal; he affirms that humorists are heroes of the periods of decline, and to prove it he wrote in a book three essays: on Petronius, Cervantes, and Machado de Assiz.

Solid, sensible Plinio Barreto has a good reputation not only as a literary critic but also as a jurist. Sergio Milliet is a man of good taste and an aesthetician who writes on men, books, and ideas but who has a particular liking for artistic subjects. Sousa Filho incidentally reviews books, but sociology and philosophy are the provinces of thought where he really feels at home.

A mature man in his late twenties, Antonio Candido is one of the most penetrating and comprehensive critics of modern Brazil. It is true delight to read his book reviews.

My country is today very rich in columnists. Unlike the American ones, they generally do not write about international affairs. They are chiefly interested in men and problems of their country, and not seldom they get into tremendous arguments with one another.

One of the most popular among them is Genolino Amado, a very talented writer who writes daily for newspapers, magazines, and radio programs. The range of subjects he treats is amazingly wide.

Brave, outspoken, and intelligent Osorio Borba is the author of "The Literary Comedy." Rubem Braga has a style of his own and he is full of brotherly feelings toward the lower classes; in his book "The Count and the Little Bird" there are true masterpieces of ironic fantasy.

One of the greatest humorists of the Portuguese language is Apporely (pen name of Apparicio Torelly). His humor is a kind of combination of the French *esprit* with the Anglo-American sense of humor and the Spanish picaresque. I hope that in the future critics will understand the real importance of this writer.

As for the journalists—I mean the editors and directors of newspapers—conspicuous among them is prolific, terrific, infernally intelligent Assiz Chateaubriand, a daring entrepreneur, a kind of Brazilian Hearst; he writes daily his syndicated column, where he derides or praises politicians and tackles almost all imaginable subjects. André Carrazoni, a former Parnassian poet, is a journalist still in love with form, and his editorials are sometimes wonderful literary pieces. Brave, clear-minded Macedo Soares is another widely read and admired journalist. A man of few words and restrained irony is Costa Rego. Famous is Mauricio de Medeiros' column in São Paulo's "Gazeta." Late Lindolfo Collor was considered one of the best political commentators of Brazil. And the small but pleasant column of Austregésilo de Atahyde is released throughout the country in more than twenty newspapers.

Travel books are not abundant in Brazil. (The explanation is quite simple: writers in my country are generally men who cannot afford to travel.) Among the few noteworthy ones are Monteiro Lobato's "America," Dante Costa's "Paris," Jayme A. da Camara's narrative of his travels through Scandinavia, Herman Lima's description of "Skies and Lands of Europe," and Claudio de Sousa's book on the East.

Now we come to the scanty dramatic harvest. Joracy Camargo scored a hit with his "God Bless You!"—which was translated into many languages and staged even in Russia. "Maria Cachucha," "The Jackass," and "The Savant" are among his many successful plays. Camargo is an author with a taste for the discussion of the philosophy of life. He has an astounding facility for writing dialogue. The major interest of his plays lies in conversation rather than in plot. Brilliant, sometimes paradoxical, always a perfect technician, he is one of the most famous of Brazilian playwrights.

Ernani Fornari, who is also a poet and a novelist of good reputation, confesses to have found his real spiritual climate in dramatic literature. Starting his career as a playwright with a moving and rather pessimistic play called "Nothing," which met with considerable success, he later on took Rio and São Paulo by storm with his comedy of costumes "Iaiá Boneca." It is a delicate and well-written play of family life in the middle eighties; it has a touch of sentimentality and romance, and its background is historical. Fornari's last hit was a dramatic play whose action takes place in the land of Gauchos, in the days of one of the bitterest Brazilian civil wars.

Maria Jacinta writes plays on modern city life, and she is more concerned with moral and social issues, with society's prejudices, and with psychological problems. A really fine playwright who abhors sensationalism and who is very punctilious as to characterization, she has written such fine plays as "The Taste of Life" and "Conflict."

Plotful and pleasant are the works of Oduvaldo Vianna, whose comedy "Love" was a smash hit in both Brazil and Argentina.

"The River," by Carlos de Lacerda, is an impressive play much in the line of "Tobacco Road" but with an emphasis on the dramatic rather than on the grotesque.

Raymundo Magalhães had a great success with his clever historical plays—chiefly with "A Jew," which was inspired by an episode in Disraeli's life.

Renato Vianna, himself an actor, is a competent technician with a taste for transcendent themes, as we easily can see from the titles of some of his plays: "God," "Sex," "Jesus Is Knocking at Our Door." His plays are eloquently written and solidly constructed.

Oswald de Andrade's social plays are full of allegories and their humor has a surrealist quality. They remind you of Saroyan's works, but you must not forget that when they were written Saroyan, still a very young man, had not yet started writing for the theater. And, speaking of Saroyan, it occurs to me that Oswald de Andrade is in our literature a kind of aerialist, always the "daring young man on the flying trapeze." A bold experimentalist, a man in love with intellectual adventures, he is never afraid to turn somersaults in the air.

And now from my house on Fulton Street, San Francisco, California, trying to overcome space and time, I project my gaze on the Brazilian literary scene, in order to see if I have overlooked some writer of importance. Yes, there I see one. How have I forgotten him? The only explanation is that I like him too much. His name? Alvaro Moreyra. He is a stout short fellow with a curving nose, a fleshy face, and big shell-rimmed spectacles. He writes in undertones. He is ironical, yes, but he is also full of tenderness. He imitates nobody, but he is very much imitated. He lives in a universe of his own, which does not mean he lives in an ivory tower. Not at all. He is concerned with human problems. He loves human beings. His wife, Eugenia, is a talented actress of artistic gifts. The Moreyras' home is informal, Bohemian, always swarming with noisy interesting people—sons, daughters, sons-in-law and daughters-in-law, friends, relatives, and not seldom completely unknown persons who enter without being invited and who never are asked questions but are treated like old acquaintances. The whole atmosphere is reminiscent of that house in the Kaufman-Hart comedy "You Can't Take It with You."

Alvaro Moreyra's natural means of expression is not the poem or the novel and not even the short story. I find no exact name for his writings, which sometimes resemble mere jottings in an intimate notebook. They are delicious pieces of writing, true prose poems. Sometimes they have a sarcastic tang, and even when they sound like simple anecdotes they have always a deeper meaning.

Here is one of Moreyra's little things. I quote from memory.

When Christ summoned Lazarus from among the dead, he asked him:
"Lazarus, what did you see beyond the grave?"
The resurrected man's eyes were vacant and full of amazement.
"I saw absolutely nothing, my Lord."
Christ murmured hastily:
"Is that so? Well, keep still about it, will you?"

And here I close this chapter with the vague sensation that I have just finished copying a telephone directory. . . .

XI

Between God and the Underdog

IF I had to sum up in one short sentence the main trends of Brazilian literature today, I would say that it oscillates between two poles: God and the underdog. What I mean by such an oversimplified classification is that poets and story-tellers in my country are either preoccupied with the destiny of the soul, with sin and the ultimate meaning of existence, or concerned with the living conditions of the poor classes and with social justice. The result is two different kinds of literature: one subjective and the other objective—one rather metaphysical, walking in the realm of mystery; the other positively physical, concerned with the "human document" and having in many cases political implications. Not seldom you find subjective and religious writers worrying about social problems, and leftist poets and prose writers with spiritualistic tendencies.

Vinicius de Moraes—whom Waldo Frank considers one of Brazil's best poets—writes a definitely high-brow kind of poetry, but he never loses contact with daily realities. His crude poem on the old red-light district of Rio is an impressive piece of poetry and at the same time has a tremendous social significance.

Francisco Karam's fine collection of poems, "The Thick Hour," reveals a bard who is a mixture of angel and faun. Sexless are Paulo Corrêa Lopes' religious poems; but they have a simple and sincere beauty, being the voice of a man who suffered deeply.

The verses by Carlos Drummond de Andrade are masterpieces of irony and he knows how to take out of daily events and people motives of poetry.

In "La Possession du Monde" he tells how a group of celebrities is visiting Rio. They praise the landscape, out of a sense of duty; some of them take the risk of going to the prostitution district, but others merely go to the Sugar Loaf; only Georges Duhamel spends the morning sitting on a stone and looking at the papaya trees in the back yard near the poet's house. Presently the French author rises to his feet—interrupting an erudite scientific dissertation of his friend, an eminent neurologist. The poet continues:

> *Maybe he was going to deliver the message of Europe*
> *To the enslaved hearts of young America. . . .*
> *But he just pointed to the papaya tree*
> *And asked for* ce cocasse fruit jaune.

Drummond de Andrade's "Literary Policy" is a satire on the silly feuds of literary circles.

> *The municipal poet*
> *discusses with the state poet*
> *about which of the two is capable of licking*
> *the federal poet.*
>
> *Meanwhile the federal poet*
> *takes gold out of his nose.*

Now I realize that Drummond de Andrade's poems which I have just quoted are noncommittal as regards either God or the underdog, which proves that it is easier to classify butterflies than poets.

Jorge de Lima, Murillo Mendes and Adalgisa Nery belong to the same spiritual climate. Their poetry is a mixture of Biblical allegories (mainly in the style of the Song of Songs and Ecclesiastes), Freudian symbols, and surrealist images.

Jorge de Lima decided to "restore poetry in Christ." From his "The Seamless Tunic" comes this poem.

POETRY IS HIGHER

I want to build the temple, the great temple, I want materials,
I want to make the altar for the holocaust and for incense.
I will burn the useless perfumes in God's nostrils,
In the hair of the archangel, in the breath of all the elect.
I want eighty thousand arms to demolish hills and to fell woods,
And some three hundred thousand persons to get pure water.
I want one to divine where there is gold, where is the sun.
Get me a robber to steal the moon.
Come, sculptor, and make a cherub with three-span wings,
  holding a huge cup and a bronze palm.
And upon the column thou shalt place a flying fish,
  flying to I don't know where.
Call Solomon to sweep the temple with his wisdom
  and with his thousand wives, with his mares and with his crook.
And afterward let the fire from heaven come to burn the offer-
  ings
And let all things fall with their faces to the earth,
Because poetry is much higher
  above you, O world so very small!

Murillo Mendes at times strikes me as a combination of Salvador Dali, Saint John the Evangelist, and D. H. Lawrence. He states that

> *White forms of archangels are moving*
> *In disorderly processions within myself,*
>   *outside myself.*

Love and eroticism, with its anatomical correspondences— womb, breasts, hips, legs, lips—and such analogical ideas as virginity, birth, pain, penetration, occur very frequently in his poems. He says that the "world began in Jandira's breasts," and that

Light is born in Eve's eyes
Night is born in Eve's hair
My parents are born in Eve's womb
I am born in Eve's womb
My beloved is born in Eve's womb.

When he talks to his beloved he gives vent to a curious kind of anxiety . . .

I never saw your mother
How is your mother?

Or . . .

I saw the girl growing
In the shadow of her mother.

Angels and archangels people the impressive verses of Murillo Mendes, and sometimes they mix with airplanes or drive fast automobiles through a timeless heaven. And, surprisingly enough, such tricks, far from achieving a grotesque effect, rather add to the mystery of the poems. Murillo Mendes himself is sometimes alternately an angel and a devil. God and sex seem to be the two magnetic poles of his unrestful complex being. Sometimes he seems to hint that sex is one of the many ways to God. With his long face, his sparkling dark eyes, and his full lips, Murillo Mendes reminds me of a Spanish monk of the Middle Ages painted by Zurbarán.

Adalgisa Nery, whose poems have a disturbing quality, is obsessed with her own body. She is constantly writing on her eyes, her breasts, her hands, her lips, her flesh. . . . Her poetry is ridden by a warm wind of mystery, and her "The Absent Woman" is a suggestive book.

Manoel Bandeira mixes tenderness and irony in his verses. Suffering from tuberculosis, far from trying to conceal his ailment, he makes fun of it, writing not seldom on hemoptysis and pneumothoraxes. In one of his poems you find the following dialogue between doctor and patient.

"So, Doctor, is it not possible to try a pneumothorax?"
"No. The only thing to do is to have an Argentine tango played."

In one of his most significant poems he says he is going away to Pasárgada, a marvelous country whose king is a friend of his and where he can get the woman he wants. Pasárgada is such a deliciously inconsequential place that there Juana, the mad queen of Spain (who happened not to be mad at all), was a relative of the daughter-in-law that he, the poet, never had. What does this Pasárgada mean? Is it the wonderful magic land of make-believe where poets and artists find rest and consolation, escaping from this drab world? It may be childhood and innocence. Nostalgia for childhood is very common among Brazilian poets. Sometimes it is symbolized by the moon, by a passing cloud or a star. Manoel Bandeira exclaims:

> *I want the morning star,*
> *Where is the morning star?*
> *My friends and my enemies*
> *Look for the morning star.*

And in the end he declares:

> *Pure or degraded to extreme baseness,*
> *I want the morning star.*

According to many a critic the most distinguished of all modern Brazilian poets is Augusto Frederico Schmidt. I, too, think that he is really a great poet, as well as a most remarkable character. Like G. K. Chesterton he is corpulent,

Catholic, cultured, and clever. His soul is a well of contradictory impulses. Schmidt is a competent businessman and a fine artist. (Could you imagine Henry J. Kaiser writing—between the launching of two ships—modern poetry with a touch of mysticism?) He is a greedy man and an ascetic, an angel and a demon. And Brazilian poetry attained its heights of subtle and mysterious beauty in the best of Schmidt's poems contained in such books as "The Blind Bird," "The Song of the Night," "Unknown Sea," and "The Lone Star."

I must confess—to close this informal dissertation on poetry—that my favorite poets are Cecilia Meirelles and Mario Quintana. What in my opinion makes them especially remarkable is their fine sense of wording. They manage to be different and not seldom profound while using simple vocables. I think their secret lies in the way they combine words so as to give them a new force, a new meaning. Though modern, their poems have a classic flavor and oftentimes they remind us of medieval ballads.

Cecilia Meirelles tells us that she sings

> . . . *because this very moment exists*
> *and my life is completed.*
> *I am not gay nor sad:*
> *I am just a poet.*
>
> *Brother of the passing things,*
> *I feel no joy or torment,*
> *I go through nights and days*
>   *in the wind.*
>
> *Whether I demolish or build,*
> *Whether I stay or vanish,*
> *I don't know, I don't know, I stay*
>   *or go.*
>
> *All I know is that I sing.*
> *The song is everything.*

It has an eternal blood, and a rhythmic wing.
One day I am sure I shall be silent
and nothing more.

Mario Quintana is a quiet timid Bohemian who lives in a world of his own making. He does not care about publishing books or having readers. He is half a human being and half an elf. From the moon, where he lives, sometimes he sends down to us songs like this.

AUTUMN SONG

Autumn plays a hand organ
In the patio of my life,
An old song, always the same,
Under my closed window.

Sorrow? Enchantment? Desire?
How can we possibly know?
A painful, uncertain joy,
As from a rough caress.

To depart, O soul, who knows?
To enjoy the hours, in brief.
But the roads of autumn
Lead us to nowhere.

In her "Epitaph for the Steerwoman" Cecilia Meirelles tells the reader that if he is asked who was that woman who lost her eyes in the godless seas of life, and who suffered from beauty and never had a surprise in her illumined face, he must answer:

. . . I could not know her,
and her story was mistold.

But her name of ship and star
was "The Serene and Desperate."

In his "Poem for New Year's Day" Quintana describes a surrealistic scene.

> *The angels sweep the bats,*
> *Throwing them into the sea. . . .*
>
> *The bells dance in the air,*
> *From house to house the roofs,*
> *Hither and thither,*
> *Exchange winged messages,*
> *Tracing frights in the air.*
>
> *Silences. Bells. Callings. Bells.*
> *And bells. Bells. And bells. Bells.*
> *Criers. Bells. Laughter. Bells.*
> *And carried by the bells,*
> *All blown by the bells,*
> *The town dances in the air!*

Both Cecilia Meirelles and Quintana like to sing about sick boys and little kings. Their poems are full of representatives of the fauna and flora of the sea—fishes, anemones, algae, coral, shells—and of the flora and fauna of the skies—the moon, stars, clouds, angels. Both poets love water, ships, silvery nocturnal landscapes, and they both seem to have no use for bright colors and grandiloquent words. Their poems have an essential limpidity; and cool cleansing winds blow through them, smelling of long distances and mysterious lands.

However, it is in the literature of fiction that the boundary lines which divide the two provinces—that of the worshipers of God and that of the knight errants of the lower classes— are more clearly and strongly traced. But before proceeding to the next chapter, in which I intend to give you a general idea of Brazilian fiction as representative of national and regional problems and aspects of today, I want to describe to you sketchily the politico-social events in my country after the revolution of October, 1930. They have affected literature to a considerable degree. In a certain measure they *are* literature too. Besides, no writer can escape history. He either helps to make it or he *suffers* it, even when he thinks he is completely detached from political and social issues.

In 1932 the *paulistas*, alleging that Getulio Vargas had stayed too long as provisional President, made a counter-revolution to eject him from power and to restore the country to a normal republican life. The federal garrisons of the state of São Paulo joined the revolutionary forces, and for nearly three months the *paulistas* maintained against the rest of the country a true war in which modern weapons—tanks, planes, machine guns, etc.—were used on a large scale. The rebel state was finally defeated after a gallant fight in which the inhabitants gave proof of tenacity and courage. There were of course economic reasons at the roots of that revolution, and it is even said that foreign capital had a share in it. But the main source of energy and power of the *paulistas* in that struggle was their sense of superiority and of tradition. Back in 1929 one of their deputies, referring to the other states of Brazil, said that "São Paulo was a locomotive pulling twenty empty wagons." São Paulo is really the most advanced of all the states of Brazil, and it is the most powerful and important industrial center in South America. Hygiene, education, and public services are better there than in the rest of the country. The *paulistas* complained that after the revolution of 1930 they had been treated not only roughly but also with a certain contempt by the provisional President. Their pride had been hurt, and also their economy.

Peace came, and in 1934 Vargas gave the nation a consti-

tution. Everything seemed to be settled. Deputies and senators engaged in their endless and sometimes futile discussions.
Some novelists and columnists were writing books which
depicted the living conditions of the lower classes, and they
clamored—even if not in plain words—for social justice.

Meanwhile Plinio Salgado, the leader of the green-shirted
fascists, went on in his campaign, getting more and more
followers. At that time many Catholics were convinced that
Mussolini was one of the pillars of the Church, and consequently they either joined the *Integralista* ranks or were
benevolent toward them. One of the pet execrations of the
fascists was Soviet Russia, and they attacked the socially
conscious writers of Brazil as communists. Their motto was
"God, Country, and Family," to which the leftists replied
with "Bread, Land, and Freedom."

In those days, when the United States followed the "dollar
policy" toward South America, Germany started to imper-
sonate the Lorelei, trying to lure Brazil with her sweet voice
and promising songs. But the whole affair transcended the
realm of pure music and poetry. The German businessmen
backed those songs with something concrete, offering
Brazilian firms first-rate goods at convenient prices and conditions. They did that clicking their heels, and with a polite
smile on their rubicund faces. The Brazilian merchants were
delighted and preferred to do business with Germany rather
than with the United States. And when you asked them the
reason for that they answered that the Germans were more
friendly and gave them long-term credit. And so political
propaganda entered Brazil, goose-stepping through the door
of commercial relations. There were more than half a million
Germans in the southern part of my country. They were
generally prosperous farmers and big shots of the industrial
world. They had their athletic clubs and glee clubs, their
schools and beer halls; and, as long as they lived in suburbs

or cities of their own, many of them never learned Portuguese properly or at all.

What did our government do about the whole German problem? To begin with, our former rulers did not see the thing as a "problem." They left the Germans to themselves, alleging that they were industrious and peace-loving. But the real reason was that the Germans insisted on being just Germans, and on teaching their Brazilian-born children that their real fatherland was Germany. The main intention of our government being not to promote the welfare of the nation, but simply to stay in power, they made a strange and dangerous deal with the Germans, even if such an agreement was never written. They would let the Germans alone to do what they pleased as long as at election time they would all vote for the official candidates. And so, amid the indifference and blindness of the politicians of the old regime, the Germans grew strong in Brazil, constituting a dangerous ethnological island or, to use a less poetical image, "a racial cyst."

Then Hitler came, and with him Goebbels and his infernal propaganda machine. The glee and athletic clubs and other apparently harmless societies became political-minded. Brazilian branches of the Nazi party were founded. They held secret as well as public meetings in which they wore brown shirts with the swastika symbol. They paraded along the streets in military fashion, and of course they found in the Brazilian fascists enthusiastic allies. The green shirts aimed at the destruction of communism in the country and the abolishment of external debts. They were fanatically nationalistic and mildly anti-Jewish. The Nazis, with their hatred of Soviet Russia and their undisguised enmity for the Anglo-American plutocrats, suited the *Integralistas* well. In Brazil no Communist party was (or is) allowed to exist. The other political groups were old-fashioned, theoretical-minded, and too much preoccupied with innocuous speeches and the grabbing of good official positions and favors. So the only active party with revolutionary impetus and a semimilitary organization in the land was the *Integralista*.

In 1935 there was a military rebellion in Rio de Janeiro, and among its leaders there were some army officers with leftist ideas. The movement failed completely and had no popular support. The rebels were crushed in a few hours. Later on, the secret police of Rio arrested, in his hiding place in one of the suburbs of the city, Luiz Carlos Prestes, who with many other leaders of the coup was tried and condemned to a long term in prison. Ironically enough, such a leftist revolution helped the rightist plans enormously. The Brazilian fascists took all the advantage they could of that uprising. They cried: "Join the *Integralista* ranks in this sacred war against the communist barbarians who are planning to destroy our country, our families, and our sacred traditions!" And they won more and more adepts. They now were thousands and thousands throughout Brazil. They were planning to take the government through a *coup d'état*. People were convinced that the nation was going fascist; and events reached a climax the day President Vargas was seen side by side with the Brazilian *Integralista* leader, smiling down on the green-shirted militia which passed on the street in a military parade.

Vargas had promised to hold elections for President in 1937. The states of São Paulo and Rio Grande do Sul joined hands and nominated their candidate. Another group—and among them many intellectuals—nominated for President the novelist José Americo de Almeida. Both sides started heavy political propaganda: posters, broadcasts, speeches, booklets—the old routine. And one fine day in November, 1937, the nation was surprised with the news of a spectacularly successful *coup d'état*. Getulio Vargas had been overthrown by Getulio Vargas. He had dissolved all political parties (including the *Integralista*), closed the senate and the house of deputies, and voted a new constitution made especially to fit his *Estado Novo,* "new state." To do that he counted on the support of the army, and the main reason alleged for such an extreme measure was the necessity of avoiding extremes; that is to say, communism and fascism.

The following year the *Integralistas* tried a dramatic coup that almost succeeded. They attacked the President's residential palace, killed many of the guards; and during almost two hours Vargas, his brother, and a group of loyal friends, including his brave daughter Alzira, shot at the aggressors, until reinforcements came—which relieved the siege and killed or arrested the *Integralistas*.

There followed months of relative tranquillity in which the country was trying to adapt itself to the new regime.

So came 1939 and the second World War. Some military men around Vargas were much fascinated by the power of the German army. Norway, Belgium, and Holland were invaded. The gods of war seemed to favor Hitler's soldiers. In June, 1940, France fell. The victory of Germany seemed indisputable. The United States was out of the war, and the isolationists were working hard to keep the country neutral. Brazil had a strong German population. Hitler would sooner or later create a minority case regarding her, like that of Sudetenland. The Brazilian army was not strong enough to oppose the Wehrmacht. Everything indicated that Brazil was marching into Germany's zone of influence, as a satellite country. Vargas was not pro-German, but he was a realist and he would do what he thought best for the country.

Meanwhile what did the Brazilian people think of the war? They were decidedly pro-United Nations. Writers expressed their ideas through newspaper articles, interviews, and speeches. The majority believed that Brazil had to participate in the fight to crush the totalitarian menace in the world. And so Germany started to sink neutral ships indiscriminately. Her submarines sent some Brazilian ships to the bottom of the sea. People in my country were angry. There were demonstrations in the streets against German property. One strong pro-United Nations voice, that of Oswaldo Aranha, Brazilian Minister of Foreign Affairs, spoke out. The good-neighbor policy started by the Roosevelt government, and successfully carried out by the Department of State and the Coordinator of Inter-American Affairs, was producing its fruits in terms of a better understanding and close friendship between the two countries. Led by Aranha, Brazil broke her diplomatic relations with Germany and Italy and, later on, declared war on those two nations. Everybody knows the important role played by the Natal air·base in the battle of Africa.

All those disturbances in Brazil prior to 1939 were followed by periods of suspicion, unrest, and strict censorship. I need not say that censorship is ruinous to literature. From 1930 to 1936 the harvest in the field of fiction had been unusually rich; but from 1937 on it declined, if not in quantity, at least in quality. I am sure that the reason for such an impoverishment is mainly political.

The position of the Brazilian intellectuals of today may be summed up in this way. There is a group of leftist writers who desire a democratic government with emphasis on socialism, and who are fighting on behalf of a world of international cooperation on a basis of Roosevelt's four freedoms. On the other hand the Catholic writers, who think that the whole problem is of a spiritual nature, are much concerned not only with the defeat of Nazi Germany but also with the annihilation of Soviet Russia; at the same time some of them eye with distrust United States gestures of friendship toward

Brazil, because they think that "Yankee morality and materialistic civilization" (as expressed by some moving pictures in terms of heavy drinking, divorces, money-making, etc.) are very dangerous to Brazilian Catholic traditions. Some Catholics would like to have in Brazil a regime like that of Franco in Spain. A not very large group of intellectuals merely contemplate a return to good old liberal democracy, and a kind of laissez-faire regime. And of course there are always the touch-me-not lodgers of the ivory tower who simply ignore social issues.

Nowadays things political and literary tend to a frightful simplification. You light a candle either to the Pope or to Stalin. I think it is disgraceful when people lose their sense of shading. In my opinion a writer should not belong to political parties, because the urge to follow party lines at all times will undoubtedly ruin his work.

On the other hand there is not much point in behaving like the fellow who had a private tommy gun and who, having been asked during the Spanish civil war what side he was fighting for, answered: "None. I fight on my own account."

The Patchwork Quilt

WHAT is the most representative novel of Brazil?

To answer this question properly you need first of all to find out what is the most representative region or human group of my country, and I do not believe that in justice you could arrive at a definite choice. It has been said that the true Brazilian novel would be one capable of covering the whole national geographic and human landscape from the Atlantic seaboard to the wilderness of Mato Grosso and from the rolling fields of Rio Grande do Sul to the Amazonian jungle. We do not yet have such an ambitious novel; and if we had I do not think it could be very good, because its enormous expanse would spoil its profundity and such a book would certainly be more geographic and picturesque than human and sociologically significant.

I think that the great mural of Brazil is being painted today not by one artist alone but by scores of them. Every one of our modern novelists is working in his limited field—a social group, a city, a state, a region—and, putting their works together, you will have the vast panoramic fresco of the nation.

Look at the map of Brazil. What do you see? A land with the shape of a Virginia ham and with more than a score of states, each of them painted in a different color. I guess what you are thinking. . . . You are right: Brazil looks like a patchwork quilt.

With a surface of 3,290,564 square miles, it has frontiers with all South American countries excepting Ecuador and

Chile. Her population is about forty-five million inhabitants. Her territory is a vast flat plateau limited by high mountain ranges near the Atlantic shores. As you proceed inland, the plains slope down toward the depression formed by the great Amazon and Paraguay rivers. Seven-tenths of the Brazilian territory are covered by forests, of which some eight hundred thousand square miles are thick jungle.

The Amazon region is a land of nightmare beyond description. It has a primitive and tragic kind of beauty. The soul of its inhabitants oscillates feverishly between two fascinating horrors: the jungle and the river. Swarming with all kinds of fish, alligators, and snakes, the river sometimes undermines its red banks, causing them to fall with their huts, plantations, human beings, and domestic animals. At certain periods of the year the Amazon, like a roaring white cobra, pushes violently against the sea in a wave fifty feet high which sweeps before it everything it encounters. The waters invade the forest and the plains, producing swamps which in their turn are the source of millions of mosquitoes which bite men—causing their skin to grow sore and swell and leaving in their blood the microbe of malarial fever. And the same intermittent fever oftentimes seems to take possession of the trees, the waters, the animals, and even the sun. The Amazon is a kind of damp green inferno full of surprises, wonders, and frights. In the entangled forest you mistake the boa constrictors, whose embraces are fatal, for lianas, and you never know whether a plant can heal or kill you.

In the times of the rubber boom, men entered the jungle and stayed there for a long time milking the precious rubber trees. They faced all kinds of dangers and hardships, and those who survived emerged from the jungle to sell their rubber for high prices. They made a lot of money and began spending it madly, having a "hell of a good time" drinking champagne in Manaus—the capital city of the Amazon—and buying jewels and expensive dresses for their wives, daughters, or mistresses. They usually spent in short weeks what they had earned in months of toil and suffering.

One day a mysterious English gentleman managed to smuggle out of the country some rubber tree seeds, and England started her plantations in Singapore. The Brazilian rubber lost most of its markets; its prices fell, and that meant bankruptcy for the *seringueiros*. And today—as one of the vestiges of an epoch of luxury and prodigality—you find in the poor colonial-looking Manaus a magnificent opera house, one of the most imposing in South America.

Nature seems to be the central character in the short stories and novels of the Amazon. Our literature about that region has not much of the exuberance, strength, and color of its subject. It is rather scanty, because it is not easy to go to the Amazonian forest; and to stay there is still harder. Few writers in Brazil are endowed with an adventurous soul, and to enter the jungle is always a risky adventure.

A steamboat skipper for thirty years, Raymundo de Morais knew the "big river" like the palms of his own hands. His books "Letters from the Forest" and "In the Amazon Plain" are packed with valuable information and interesting descriptions.

Delightful is the book which Vianna Moog wrote on "The Cycle of Black Gold." He is a sophisticated European-minded writer giving in limpid prose his impressions of a primitive land and people.

Fiction about the Amazon is not abundant nowadays.

Peregrino Junior wrote a couple of books of short stories in which in an unpretentious and charming way he describes landscapes, men, habits, of that prodigious country.

Gastão Cruls' "The Mysterious Amazon Region" is a

highly readable novel which the author wrote without ever having been to the Amazon. Later on, after actually visiting the "green hell," the same writer published another book, "The Amazon Which I Saw"; but some critics and experts on the matter affirm that the fictional work is much more impressive than the factual one.

The Nordeste, or Northeast, is an intriguing and expressive region of Brazil. It comprises about four states of the northern seaboard. From that section came the most outspoken, elemental, and revolutionary novelists of the country.

While the southern part of Brazil was still a desolate wilderness, there existed already in Pernambuco a swarming feudal society. The Nordeste is mainly agricultural, and even today you find there clear vestiges of the feudal regime. Sugar is its chief product, and by the history of sugar cane you could trace in parallel the social history of that region.

Crossed by two rivers, Recife—the most important of the northeastern cities—is known as the "Brazilian Venice." It has a charm of its own. Its streets, churches, buildings, squares, and parks have color and character. Recife and the neighboring Olinda are historically perhaps the two most significant places in the country. Their stones and landmarks speak in romantic undertones of the Portuguese colonists and the Dutch invaders.

No one studied the Nordeste with more passion and accuracy than sociologist Gilberto Freyre. He tells us in his books of the influence of the Portuguese, the Negro, and the Indians on the Northeastern society; he analyzes very acutely all the elements of that bewildering melting pot. Folklore, history, art, cooking, country and city life, genealogical trees—Freyre writes of them all in his endeavor to describe, understand, and explain his Nordeste.

His counterpart in the field of fiction is José Lins do Rego, one of the foremost Brazilian novelists of today. In a series of books with the general title of "The Cycle of Sugar Cane," he narrates the story of a "sugar mill boy," of his education in a boarding school in Recife, of his coming of age, and of his thoughts, emotions and adventures on the day he had to take the place of his dead grandfather as the master of the family sugar mill. Those stories are written in a very personal manner by a deft writer who has the power of making us believe in everything he tells. Lins do Rego focused in his novels many other aspects of Northeastern life. His characters are true to life. His writing at times is careless, but it has ever the flavor of a picturesque fireside talk.

One of the most tragic problems of some sections of the Northeast is the periodical droughts which cause entire populations to migrate under the most piteous conditions. Deeply impressed by such calamities, José Americo de Almeida published in 1928 a novel—"A Bagaceira"—in which he describes one of those dramatic hegiras. The story is somber; the scenery is barren; the characters are poor souls ravaged by the drought, which makes them seem like walking corpses. The story, written with vigor and frankness, impressed readers and critics powerfully. Its author may be considered one of the pioneers of the social novel of Brazil.

Less than two years later a girl under twenty—Raquel de Queiroz—published "The Year Fifteen," a surprisingly mature story whose backdrop is the tremendous drought of 1915. The novel has no romantic touch; it is plotless and rather dry. But how pungent is its meaning, how deep and ominous are its implications!

However, most parts of the Nordeste are not ravaged by droughts. Nature there is not so imposing and ferocious as in the Amazon. Northeastern people and habits are rather different. Not having the forest or the river to fight, the

nordestinos fight one another. Illiteracy and bad health
among the lower classes breed fanaticism and banditry. The
backlands are infested by groups of brigands who loot and
kill in farms and villages. It is said that many of those desper-
adoes rob the rich to give to the poor, like rough bronzed
Robin Hoods. The living standard in the Northeastern
towns is generally low. Of course there are gentle and lovable traits in the life of those communities. People there, as
in the rest of the country, are kind and hospitable. They
have rather patriarchal habits, inherited from the Portuguese.
There is a certain charm in those small towns of cobbled or
unpaved streets, dejected-looking houses with dejected-
looking girls at their windows, and on the plaza the little
Catholic church in whose diminutive belfry owls nest. The
mayor and political chief of the town has invariably the
honorary title of colonel, and he is the indisputable local
boss. Another figure of prestige is the Catholic vicar. Life is
calm, monotonously even, in those cities. But of course there
are dramas—not complicated psychological ones; nothing
for a Joyce, a Proust, or a Mauriac. But there is plenty of
meat for an Erskine Caldwell or a James T. Farrell. That
very dreariness and lack of drama is dramatic enough. And
you have poverty, injustice, prostitution, greed, hate, envy,
love—all the elementary passions. Yes, and sometimes traditional rivalry between families explodes into true bloody
"wars."

Expressive of that kind of life and humanity are the novels
by Graciliano Ramos, one of the most solid and profound
of all Brazilian writers of today. He is himself a somber and
embittered person, because he lived during more than forty
years amid that type of people and problems and he suffered
in mind and in flesh much violence, injustice, and slow
horror. He is a notable storyteller. His style is dry, precise,
and correct. "Anguish" is the name of a masterful psycho-

logical novel which tells the story of a submerged character living in one of the Northeastern towns, and a victim of all those disgraceful circumstances. Not so somber, but still bitter, is another book of his—"São Bernardo"—very expressive of the country life and people of the Nordeste.

Raquel de Queiroz wrote three more novels, and very good ones, whose setting is her native state of Ceará. One of them is a daring psychological study of a murderer—a rough, illiterate man of the country. The action takes place within the cell in which the criminal is imprisoned, or, if you prefer, within his own mind.

Luiz Jardim, a painter and designer of note, tried his hand successfully in a book of short stories—"Dangerous Maria" —whose characters and settings belong to his native Pernambuco.

Many of the capital cities of those Northeastern states are far from being rich, stimulating, or progressive. In "The Corumbas," Amando Fontes, a restrained novelist who has not much use for adjectives, narrates the story of a poor country couple who moved to the capital city of their state in search of a better life but who found pain and shame instead. In a sequel, "Siriri Street," Fontes described life in the prostitutes' quarter of the same city.

The same situation to a certain extent is prevalent in the state of Bahia. But color and tropical beauty is what you find in the charming city of São Salvador da Bahia, built on a hill in front of the sea. (Those northern Brazilian seas are generally of a luminous green, their shores being white and bordered with palm trees.) That city has a great concentration of Negroes, and there you find pure Negroes or mulattoes clad in fine clothes and holding important social positions. Bahia is famous for its three hundred and sixty-five lovely churches, most of them in the Portuguese colonial style. Famous, too, are its songs; its cooking; its colorful black mammies who sell African candies, cakes, and cookies along the streets, displaying gaudy dresses.

Bahia found its rhapsodist in Jorge Amado, one of the most talented Brazilian novelists. This young man is a born storyteller. He has no love or respect for grammar: he writes as he pleases. But how! His prose is fluent, picturesque, and expressive. A poet at heart, sometimes his pages are pure poetry. His stories are tinged with a manly kind of lyricism. His characters are generally rough folk, stevedores, fishermen, farmers, tramps, whores, bandits; and he has special liking for the Negroes. His half a dozen excellent novels describe the life of these people. The slums of Bahia are pictured in "Sweat," and the cacao plantations in "Cacao." He tells a tale of fishermen in "Dead Sea," and of abandoned street urchins in "Captains of the Sand." His "Jubiabá" is the story of Baldo, the Negro, an ex-prize fighter, a tramp, a rhapsodist, and an ebony Casanova. It is a delightful book swept by the winds of adventure. Last year Amado published the saga of the cacao plantations of his state—"Terras do Sem Fim," a panoramic novel full of pathos and drama. It is in my opinion one of the most daring and impressive novels ever published in Brazil. It is a barbaric parade of heroes and bandits, potentates and underdogs, whores and saints, common people and ghosts. The book is at the same time a prose poem, a folkloric tale, a crude story, a libel, and a work of art.

Leaving that colorful patch of our quilt, we experience an abrupt change of temperature when we enter Minas Gerais, known as the "Brazilian Switzerland." The atmosphere is much cooler in this state, and at certain altitudes it is even freezing. The landscape is mountainous, the air clean, the sky limpid. The most important city of Minas Gerais is not yet forty years old; it has the suggestive name of "Beautiful Horizon" and it was built expressly to be the state's capital. Throughout Minas Gerais you find old traditional cities, full of memories of the times of the gold and diamond rushes, romantic colonial churches, manors, and fountains.

People in Minas Gerais are notably different from those in the other Brazilian regions. They are pious folks and rather taciturn. As politicians they proved to be sly and wise. Their country people are suspicious and sedentary.

The kind of literature produced in this interesting region is more subjective than objective. The *mineiros* are likely to be introverts rather than extroverts. Cyro dos Anjos, following the best tradition of Machado de Assiz, wrote a psychological novel which met with considerable *succès d'estime*. Lucio Cardoso is another representative writer of Minas Gerais. He has the sense of drama, he is serious, and his books make me think of a cross between Julian Green and François de Mauriac. One of our critics saw in him a potential Dostoevsky. The very titles of his books reveal his tendencies: "Subterranean Light," "Empty Hands," "The Unknown." . . .

Eerie, mysterious, and foggy are the characters and the setting of Cornelio Penna's "Frontiers." Against the background of Minas Gerais move the figures of Guilhermino Cesar's "South" and Eduardo Frieiro's "The Cape of Storms." And one of the best storytellers of the region is João Alfonsus, whose "The Blind Hen" is considered a masterpiece of Brazilian fiction.

Rio de Janeiro is the most pleasant and picturesque city I know. To begin with, the scenery is breath-taking. Nature in the Amazon kills. In Rio nature enchants; invites people to loaf, to lead a pagan life. I have never seen such a delirious display of blues, green and red and golden hues, as in the landscape around Brazil's capital city.

The *cariocas*—or inhabitants of Rio—love three things above all others: the sun, the sea, and the samba. They are themselves the most colorful and rich details of the landscape. The samba is their natural language. And they sing and dance their lives away between the green waves of the sea and the blue expanse of the sky. The *carioca* is a born loafer, an incorrigible Bohemian, and a spontaneous humorist. The best jokes in the world are made in Rio. And the city offers you a kind of tour around the world, because it has the Parisian boulevard, the ultramodern Russian city, fashionable seaside resorts in the best tradition of Biarritz or Miami, the provincial suburb—besides other aspects typically *carioca*. If you take a car downtown, in less than half an hour you can be in the forest or in the mountains; and countryside and sea are also very close at hand.

After the revolution of 1930 a great number of novelists from the provinces flocked to Rio, but paradoxically enough they did not try to write about the "city marvelous." They wrote on their home states or towns; they could not get rid of their ghosts or the bitter or sweet remembrances of their lost childhood. Their memory was peopled with the dreadful images of the droughts, the gaunt faces of their suffering countryfolk; they had dreams of social justice, or they were simply in love with native landscapes and people.

Among the most important recorders of life in Rio is Marques Rebello (pen name of Edy Dias da Cruz). He abhors those sections of his city which imitate Europe or the United States, with their skyscrapers, Coca-Cola advertisements, tourists, and so forth. He loves suburban Rio. In his novel "The Star Rises" and in many of his short stories you find the real Rio de Janeiro with its traditional life, its white-collar men and women, its old-fashioned government officers; its loafers, vendors, bourgeois, samba composers, singers, and dancers. . . .

Another book which captures the atmosphere of Rio is Eneas Ferraz' "A Carioca Family."

In Rio and São Paulo live many novelists whose works have not much to do with their cities, their emphasis being more on characterization and universal psychological problems. That is the case of Gastão Cruls, who wrote "Vertigo"; of Lucia Miguel Pereira, author of "Daybreak"; and of Gilberto Amado, whose two recent novels—"The Innocent and the Guilty Ones" and "The Interests of the Company" —caused many discussions. Oswaldo Alves had a very significant debut with his novel "A Man within the World." And one of the most distinguished virtuosi of the novel, a master technician and a very deft writer, is José Geraldo Vieira, whose "The Fortieth Door" is one of the most important novels published in Brazil recently.

Octavio de Faria's "A Bourgeois Tragedy" is an ambitious work in the vein of Jules Romain's "Les Hommes de Bonne Volonté" or Martin Du Gard's "Les Thibault." His intention, I think, is to depict the upper-middle-class life in Rio. He is a novelist who has much of the prophet concerned with sin and punishment.

In the last ten years feminine literature has been enriched with a group of names and books. Lia C. Dutra's "Ship without Port" was awarded in 1943 one of the most important literary prizes of Brazil. Tetrá de Teffé published a successful novel, "I Knocked at the Door of Life." Dinah Silveira de Queiroz' charming "Blossoms in the Sierra" was a bestseller. Friends now send me word from Brazil that a new distinguished novelist, Clarice Lispector, recently made an impressive debut. In São Paulo, Sra. Leandro Dupré's novels "The Romance of Thereza Bernard" and "We Were Six" were highly praised by critics and eagerly read by the public.

And, in the field of the short story, lively Lygia Fagundes is the most noteworthy newcomer, with her interesting book "Live Beach."

Not far from Rio, São Paulo, whose capital city reminds you sometimes of downtown Los Angeles, has a strongly Italianate population. It is a city of order, work, and speed. People there rush about in the best Yankee fashion. In Rio, men generally stay for a long time at the sidewalk cafés— sitting at tables, talking leisurely to their friends as if they had nothing to do. São Paulo's inhabitants drink hurriedly their very hot coffee, standing at the counters. São Paulo has four distinct seasons, and most of its area lies within the temperate zone.

It is an industrial as well as an agricultural state, coffee being its chief product. Its inhabitants are generally healthy-looking and their living standard is much higher than that of most states of Brazil.

If you want to know São Paulo's life and people you should pick up one of the delightful books by Antonio Alcantara Machado Filho, which swarm with lively characters typically *paulistas*. Machado was a fine humorist, an able writer, and it is really a pity he died in his middle thirties. Another remarkable storyteller is Affonso Schmitt, author of "Curiango."

And a book I recommend as representative of São Paulo's life, human types, and popular speech is "Belazartes" by Mario de Andrade.

In a previous chapter I have already told you that nobody wrote better on the *paulista* hillbilly than Monteiro Lobato. And a very delicious novel on the *paulista* countryside is "Cabocla" by Ribeiro Couto, who is also the author of many short stories on urban life—all of them simply and beautifully written.

In his novel "Plateau," Flavio de Campos moves his characters against a *paulista* background. Giving a modern version to an old Biblical story, Menotti del Picchia wrote a successful novel: "Salome."

If you want to know what life and people are like on a coffee plantation ask Luiz Martins, reading his novel "Fazenda." A proletarian "romance" is Tito Battini's "And Now What to Do?" "Beans and Dreams" by Origines Lessa is a rather bitter story of *paulista* life, the drama of a dreamer who had to worry about his daily dish of beans. Aldo Nay's "The Two Sergeants" created quite a sensation. And in Galeão Coutinho's "Simão Caolho's Memoirs" critics saw the work of a novelist who is also a fine satirist.

But it was the "daring young man on the flying trapeze," Oswald de Andrade, who attempted the most ambitious novel on São Paulo. His "Landmark Zero" is an epic of the social life of his state from 1930 on. The book is tumultuous and full of colorful characters. The style is sparkling and the intention definitely satiric.

History and environment are to a certain extent responsible for what people are in my native state of Rio Grande do Sul. That southernmost region of Brazil was the main battlefield of the country. It saw many a foreign invasion. It has been the source of many revolutions. Its inhabitants are used to warfare. Futhermore, being a cattle state, a land of ranches and cowboys, the activities of its people are generally violent.

The land is good; the landscape, gentle—rather European in appearance, with beautiful rolling green fields which impress you as a sea of petrified waves. And there is the pampa, too, the enormous expanses of grassy fields. There is no mystery in Rio Grande do Sul's landscape. There is no cosmic terror in the Gaucho souls. Rio Grande do Sul is not a region of religious people. Its folklore is rather poor; its popular music almost nonexistent. Gauchos are impetuous, a bit boisterous, but very loyal friends. It is said they are incapable of an act of treason. They never resort to ambush. They love single combat and they meet the enemy face to face, their code of honor having a strong Spanish tinge.

There is a certain similitude between the Argentine and Uruguayan Gauchos and the countryfolk of my state. The ranch life and routine, as well as much of their jargon, are almost the same. We and those neighboring populations have some habits, dreams, and legends in common. The Brazilian counterpart of the famous "Martin Fierro" is "Antonio Chimango," a delightful political satire in verse, written by Amaro Juvenal (pen name of Ramiro Barcelos). In modern times the most interesting and expressive Gaucho poems are those by Vargas Netto. And the number one storyteller of the region is Darcy de Azambuja; by that I mean that I think him first-rate as a teller of tales without any social or political preoccupations. He belongs to the good tradition of Eça de Queiroz, and many of his short stories are today included in almost all national anthologies.

Only recently writers in Rio Grande do Sul realized that their countryfolks were not only subject matter for books but human beings whose living conditions were far from being ideal. Ciro Martins, a man in love with rural life, focused social problems in a group of very commendable novels like "While the Waters Are Running," "Wandering Message," and "Closed Gate." Ivan Martins' realistic "Wild Frontier," a book which in intensity and purpose reminds us of Caldwell's "Tobacco Road," provided quite a commotion in the nation.

Urban bourgeois life is what Telmo Vergara writes about in his short stories and novels. His tales are slices of life without any preoccupation with plot. His emphasis is rather on characters and habits and psychological analysis. "The Lost Road" is the title of his most important novel. His short stories are contained in such books as "Seven Peaceful Stories" and "Chairs on the Sidewalk."

Dionelio Machado scored a hit with "The Rats," a somber novel of common life whose hero is a common man. His last book is "Desolation." Machado, a distinguished psychoanalyst, is not interested in writing beautiful pages. His style is precise, minute, and somewhat destitute of color. Not seldom he displays a Balzacian eye, and I think that his main intention as an artist is to transmit to the reader a feeling of the unusual through the very usual; in other words, to reveal the content of mystery and phantasmagoria that exists in everyday life.

A gourmet and a novelist, De Sousa Junior knows how to mix a salad and how to concoct a plot. His somber books—"Till Death Comes" and "Lightning across the Sky"—have a touch of Pirandellian mystery and are very well written.

A writer in love with form is Reinaldo Moura, whose novels emphasize the poetical and erotic side of life. Grim, bitter Pedro Wayne described country life and people in two realistic novels in which he chose to be truer to fact than to art. The odyssey of a Russian-born boy in Brazil is candidly told by Marcos Iolovitch in his novel "In a Fair April Morning."

And Vianna Moog's "A River Imitates the Rhine" is the story of a Gaucho city with a strong German population, a tale of racial pride, and a work of art which is at the same time a significant social essay.

Porto Alegre, the capital of Rio Grande do Sul, was founded by a group of Portuguese couples from the Azores. It is a lovely city with long twilights which sometimes last an hour and a half in a rich changing of colors. The German and Italian influence is strong there, but the psychological foundation of the city is Portuguese.

No one has described with more grace and exactness the lower-middle-class life of Porto Alegre than Athos Damasceno Ferreira in his novels "Black Boy" and "Little Girl." They are unpretentious pieces of literature which depict home life with a high sense of irony and at the same time with a feeling of pity and poetry. Damasceno Ferreira's style is neat, colorful, and agile.

Here we are at the end of the patchwork quilt, which, by the way, has an amazing unity in terms of a common language and of common psychological trends. Notwithstanding her enormous area, her lack of proper means of transport and communication, and the high percentage of illiteracy of her population, Brazil has one language only—the Portuguese—with no regional dialects. (Italy has over seventy different dialects.) The differences of speech among the various Brazilian regions consist mainly in intonation, and in the use of certain words or phrases typically regional which happen not to be many or too unintelligible for the inhabitants of the other sections.

Brazilians are generally a simple kind of people. Of course they have many defects, but I believe that when all is said and done you will find in them a residue of virtues. They hate war and violence, and they have no color problem. They are hospitable and kindly, even when their passionate nature causes them to seem intolerant or aggressive. (You may perhaps think that their kindness sometimes is rather aggressive.) Brazilians are Bohemian; they do not care very much about growing rich or having colossal buildings, plants, and cities. They love to loaf, and they have a wonderful sense of humor. They live more by heart than by reason.

Friendship is a magic word down there. The important thing among my people is not to be rich, commanding, or powerful, but to be *simpático;* that is to say, to be congenial, pleasant, friendly, and easygoing.

All Brazil needs is to solve her gravest and most urgent problems: illiteracy, poverty, and bad health among the lower classes. The rest is unimportant.

I do not know what is going to happen in the future. Prophecy is not my forte. But I have a great faith in the destiny of my people and my country.

It is too soon to judge our present government. We lack perspective in time. But I need no perspective either in time or in space to say very emphatically that I am all for a democratic regime with free elections, a free press, and equal opportunities for everybody; in brief, a regime capable of achieving the maximum of social welfare with the maximum of individual freedom.

As to the literature of my country—its outstanding trait of the last ten years is that Brazilian writers have ceased to be mere word jugglers, snobbish imitators of European literary fashions, or bloodless elflike dwellers of the ivory tower; they have stepped down to earth and joined hands with the common man in this universal crusade for a better world of peace, brotherhood, and freedom.

Appendix

SIXTEENTH CENTURY

Books on Brazil by Foreign Writers

Fernão Cardim	"Tratado da Terra e da Gente do Brasil"
Jean de Lery	"Histoire d'un Voyage fait en la Terre du Brésil"
Pero Lopes de Sousa	"Diario de Navegação"
Pero de Magalhães Gandavo	"Tratado da Terra do Brasil"
Pe. Manoel da Nóbrega	"Cartas do Brasil"
Pe. J. de Aspicoelta Navarro	"Cartas Jesuiticas"
Antonio Pigafeta	"Viagem ao Redor do Mundo"
Gabriel Soares de Souza	"Tratado Descritivo da Terra do Brasil"
Hans Staden	"Viagem ao Brasil"
André Thevet	"Les Singularitez de la France Antarctique"
Amerigo Vespucci	"Cartas"
Pero Vaz de Caminha	"Carta a dom Manuel, Rei de Portugal"

Books by José de Anchieta

"Informações e Fragmentos Históricos"
"Arte da Gramática da Lingua mais Usada na Costa do Brasil"
"Primeiras Letras"

SEVENTEENTH CENTURY

Representative Authors and Books

Diogo Gomes Carneiro	"Oração Apodixica"
Pe. Eusébio de Mattos	"Sermões"

Gregório de Mattos	"Obras de Gregório de Mattos" (four volumes)
Frei Vicente do Salvador	"Historia do Brasil"
Pe. Antônio Vieira	"Sermões," "Cartas"

Another representative book of the period is "Diálogo das Grandesas do Brasil," whose author is unknown.

EIGHTEENTH CENTURY

AUTHORS AND BOOKS

POETRY

Ignacio José de Alvarenga Peixoto	"Obras Poéticas"
Domingos Caldas Barbosa	"A Viola de Lereno"
Manoel Botelho de Oliveira	"A Ilha da Maré"
Claudio Manoel da Costa	"Obras"
José Basilio da Gama	"Uruguai"
Thomaz Antonio Gonzaga	"Marília de Dirceu"
Frei Manoel de Santa Maria Itaparica	"Descrição da Ilha de Itaparica"
Frei José de Santa Rita Durão	"Caramurú"
Manoel da Silva Alvarenga	"Obras Poéticas"
Antonio Pereira de Sousa Caldas	"Poesias Sacras"

PROSE

André João Antonil	"Cultura e Opulência do Brasil"
Mathias Ayres da Silva de Eça	"Reflexões Sobre a Vaidade dos Homens"
Nuno Marques Pereira	"Compêndio Narrativo do Peregrino da America"
Sebastião da Rocha Pitta	"História da América Portuguesa"

PLAYS

Antonio José da Silva   "Teatro Cômico" (two volumes)

NINETEENTH CENTURY

AUTHORS AND BOOKS OF THE PERIOD PRECEDING ROMANTICISM

POETRY

José Bonifácio de Andrade e Silva (Americo Elísio)   "Poesias"
Frei Joaquim do Amor Divino Caneca   "Obras Poeticas"

PROSE

Francisco de Monte' Alverne   "Obras Oratórias" (four volumes)
Mariano José Pereira da Fonseca (Marquês de Maricá)   "Máximas, pensamentos e Reflexões"
Bernardo Pereira de Vasconcellos   "Cartas aos Senhores Eleitos da Província de Minas Gerais"
José da Silva Lisboa (Visconde de Cairú)   "Obras Escolhidas do Visconde de Cairú"

PLAYS

Luís Carlos Martins Pena   "O Juiz de Paz na Roça"

REPRESENTATIVE AUTHORS AND BOOKS OF ROMANTICISM

POETRY

Casemiro de Abreu   "Obras Completas"
Alvares de Azevedo   "Obras" (three volumes)
Castro Alves   "Obras Completas" (two volumes)
Gonçalves Crespo   "Miniaturas," "Noturnos"
Gonçalves de Magalhães   "Suspiros Poéticos e Saudades"

Gonçalves Dias	"Obras Poéticas de Gonçalves Dias"
Teófilo Dias	"Lira dos Verdes Anos"
Fagundes Varella	"Obras Completas"
Junqueira Freire	"Obras Poéticas" (two volumes)
Francisco Octaviano	"Poesias"
Araujo Porto-Alegre	"Brasilianas"
Laurindo Rabello	"Poesias"

FICTION

José de Alencar	"Iracema," "O Guaraní," "As Minas de Prata"
Manoel Antonio de Almeida	"Memórias dum Sargento de Milícias"
Alfredo de Escragnolle Taunay	"Inocência"
Bernardo Guimarães	"A Escrava Isaura"
Joaquim Manoel de Macedo	"A Moreninha," "O Moço Louro"
Franklin Tavora	"O Cabeleira"

ESSAYS

Gal. Couto de Magalhães	"O Selvagem"
Francisco Adolfo de Varnhagen	"Historia do Brasil"

PLAYS

Joaquim José da França Junior	"As Doutoras"

REPRESENTATIVE AUTHORS AND BOOKS OF NATURALISM

FICTION

Araripe Junior (Cosme Velho)	"Miss Kate"
Aluizio de Azevedo	"A Casa de Pensão," "O Cortiço," "O Homem," "O Coruja"

Arthur Azevedo	"Contos Efêmeros"
Machado de Assiz	"Memórias Póstumas de Braz Cubas," "Quincas Borba," "Dom Casmurro," "Memorial de Ayres," "Papeis Avulsos," "Várias Historias"
José do Patrocinio	"Mota Coqueiro"
Raul Pompeia	"O Ateneu"
Julio Ribeiro	"A Carne"
Inglês de Souza	"Contos Amazônicos"
José Veríssimo	"Cenas da Vida Amazônica"

ESSAYS

Criticism, History, Biography, Sociology, Philosophy

Capistrano de Abreu	"O Descobrimento do Brazil"
Ruy Barbosa	"Discursos e Conferências," "Cartas Políticas e Literárias," "Cartas da Inglaterra," "Orações do Apóstolo," "Oração aos Moços"
Carlos de Laet	"Minha História Sagrada"
Homem de Mello	"Escritos Históricos e Literários"
Joaquim Nabuco	"Pensées Détachées," "Minha Formação"
Rocha Pombo	"História do Brasil"
Sylvio Romero	"História da Literatura Brasileira" (five volumes)
Tobias Barreto	"Estudos Alemães," "Polêmicas"

REPRESENTATIVE AUTHORS AND BOOKS OF THE PARNASSIAN POETRY

Olavo Bilac	"Poesias Completas"
Vicente de Carvalho	"Poemas e Canções"
Raymundo Corrêa	"Poesias"
Teófilo Dias	"Cantos Tropicais"
Fontoura Xavier	"Opalas"
Francisca Julia	"Esfinges"

Luíz Guimarães Filho	"Sonetos e Rimas"
Guimarães Passos	"Horas Mortas"
Machado de Assiz	"Falenas," "Crisálidas," "Americanas"
Emílio de Menezes	"Poesias"
Luíz Murat	"Poesias Escolhidas"
Alberto de Oliveira	"Poesias"
Luíz Delfino dos Santos	(No published books)
Auta de Sousa	"Horto"

REPRESENTATIVE AUTHORS AND BOOKS OF SYMBOLISM

POETRY

Alphonsus de Guimaraens	"Pastoral aos Crentes do Amor e da Morte"
B. Lopes	"Dona Carmen," "Plumário"
Felix Pacheco	"Lírios Brancos"
Mario Pederneiras	"Outono," "Rondas Noturnas"
Cruz e Sousa	"Missal," "Broqueis"

PROSE

Cruz e Sousa	"Evocações"
Gonzaga Duque	"Mocidade Morta"

BETWEEN 1900 AND 1930

POETRY

José Albano	"Redondilhas"
Guilherme de Almeida	"Messidor," "A Frauta Que Eu Perdí," "Encantamento," "Você"
Mario de Andrade	"Remate de Males," "Paulicéa Desvairada"
Oswald de Andrade	"Pau Brasil"
Augusto dos Anjos	"Eu"

Murillo Araujo	"Carrilhões"
Manoel Bandeira	"A Cinza das Horas," "Ritmo Dissoluto," "Libertinagem"
Mansueto Bernardi	"Terra Convalescente"
Zeferino Brazil	"Vovó Musa"
Humberto de Campos	"Poeira"
Ronald de Carvalho	"Poemas e Sonetos," "Luz Gloriosa," "Toda a América," "Epigramas Irônicos e Sentimentais"
Guilherme de Castro e Silva	"Alegria"
Rosalina Coelho Lisboa	"Rito Pagâo"
Da Costa e Silva	"Zodiaco"
Ribeiro Couto	"O Jardim das Confidências"
Athos Damasceno Ferreira	"Lua de Vidro"
Ascenso Ferreira	"Catimbó"
Hermes Fontes	"Lâmpada Velada"
Ernani Fornari	"Trem da Serra"
Rosário Fusco	"Poemas Cronológicos"
Paulo de Gouvêa	"Mansamente"
Eduardo Guimarães	"A Divina Chimera"
Emilio Kemp	"Poesias"
Isolino Leal	"Agua da Sanga"
Raul de Leoni	"Luiz Mediterrânea"
Jorge de Lima	"Poemas Escolhidos"
Gilka Machado	"Poemas"
Olegario Marianno	"Ultimas Cigarras," "Agua Corrente"
Cecilia Meirelles	"Nunca Mais"
Caio Mello Franco	"Vida que Passa"
Murillo Mendes	"Poemas"
Lucio de Mendonça	"Canções de Outono"
Emilio de Menezes	"Ultimas Rimas"
Augusto Meyer	"Coração Verde," "Giraluz," "Sorriso Interior"
Felipe de Oliveira	"A Lanterna Verde"
Manoelito de Ornellas	"Arco-Iris"
Menotti del Picchia	"Juca Mulato," "Máscaras," "Moisés"
Pontes de Miranda	"Inscrição da Stella Interior"

Homero Prates	"As Horas Coroadas de Rosas e Espinhos"
Cassiano Ricardo	"A Flauta de Pan," "Borrões de Verde e Amarelo," "Martim Cererê"
Augusto Frederico Schmidt	"Passaro Cego"
Julio Cesar da Silva	"A Arte de Amar"
Victor Silva	"Victórias"
Tasso da Silveira	"A Descoberta da Vida"
Adelmar Tavares	"O Caminho Enluarado"
Teodemiro Tostes	"Novena à Senhora da Graça"
Vargas Neto	"Tropilha Crioula," "Gado Chucro"
Waldemar de Vasconcellos	"A Visita das Horas Tardias"
Pedro Vergara	"Terra Impetuosa"
Alceu Wamosy	"Poesias Escolhidas"

FICTION

Moacyr de Abreu	"A Casa do Pavor"
Mateus de Albuquerque	"A Juventude de Anselmo Torres"
Medeiros e Albuquerque	"Mãe Tapuia"
Antonio de Alcantara Machado	"Laranja da China," "Braz, Bexiga e Barra Funda"
Mario de Alencar	"O que Tinha de Ser"
João Alfonsus	"Galinha Cega"
José Americo de Almeida	"A Bagaceira"
Mario de Andrade	"Amar, Verbo Intransitivo," "Macunaíma"
Oswald de Andrade	"Os Condenados"
Graça Aranha	"Canaan"
Afonso Arinos	"Pelo Sertão"
Darcy Azambuja	"No Galpão"
Odilon Azevedo	"Macegas"
Jaime Ballão Junior	"Seara Morta"
Lima Barreto	"O Triste Fim de Policarpo Quaresma," "O Escrivão Isaias Caminha," "Histórias e Sonhos"

Paulo Barreto (João do Rio)	"O Rosario da Ilusão," "Correspondência duma Estação de Cura"
Barreto Filho	"Sob o Olhar Malicioso dos Trópicos"
Albertina Bertha	"Exaltação"
Amando Caiubí	"Sapezaes e Tigueras"
Roque Callage	"Quero-Quero"
Humberto de Campos	"O Monstro e Outros Contos"
Canto e Mello	"Mana Silvéria"
Hugo de Carvalho Ramos	"Tropas e Boiadas"
Coelho Netto	"Inverno em Flor," "A Conquista," "Rei Negro," "A Tormenta"
Viriato Correia	"Novelas Doidas"
Ribeiro Couto	"O Crime do Estudante Baptista," "Bahianinha e Outras Mulheres," "Cabocla"
Gastão Cruls	"Coivara," "A Amazonia Misteriosa," "A Criatura e o Criador"
Menotti del Picchia	"Lais," "O Homem e a Morte"
Luiz Delgado	"Inquietos"
Carlos Dias Fernandes	"A Renegada"
Sebastião Fernandes	"Destinos"
Eneas Ferraz	"Uma Familia Carioca"
Ernani Fornari	"O Homem que Era Dois"
Abel Juruá	"A Veranista"
Mucio Leão	"No Fim do Caminho"
Julia Lopes de Almeida	"A Intrusa," "A Isca"
Simões Lopes Netto	"Contos Gauchescos e Lendas do Sul"
Dionélio Machado	"Um Pobre Homem"
Adelino Magalhães	"Tumulto da Vida"
Xavier Marques	"Praieiros," "Jana e Joel"
Alcides Maya	"Tapera," "Ruinas Vivas," "Almas Bárbaras"
Monteiro Lobato	"Contos Leves," "Contos Pesados"
Pedro Motta Lima	"Bruhahá"

J. A. Nogueira	"Amor Imortal"
Domingos Olympio	"Luzia Homem"
Afranio Peixoto	"A Esfinge," "Fruta do Mato," "Maria Bonita," "Bugrinha"
Vieira Pires	"Querencia"
Godofredo Rangel	"Vida Ociosa"
Plinio Salgado	"O Estrangeiro," "O Espera-do"
Antonio Salles	"Aves de Arribação"
Mario Sete	"O Palanquim Dourado," "Senhora de Engenho"
Paulo Setubal	"A Marquesa de Santos," "O Príncipe de Nassau," "As Ma-luquices do Imperador"
Waldomiro Silveira	"Os Caboclos"
Claudio de Sousa	"Mulheres Fatais"
Hilario Tácito	"Madame Pomery"
Theo Filho	"A Ilha Selvagem"
Leo Vaz	"O Professor Jeremias," "Ri-tinha"
José Vieira	"O Livro de Tilda"
José Geraldo Vieira	"A Ronda do Deslumbramen-to"

ESSAYS

Criticism, History, Biography, Sociology, Philosophy

Renato Almeida	"Fausto"
Constancio Alves	"Figuras"
Gilberto Amado	"Grão de Areia," "Aparências e Realidades"
Amadeu Amaral	"Dialeto Caipira"
Alceu de Amoroso Lima (Tristão de Atahyde)	"Afonso Arinos"
Graça Aranha	"A Estética da Vida"
Paulo Barreto (João do Rio)	"As Religiões do Rio," "A Mulher e os Espelhos"
Olavo Bilac	"Cronicas e Novelas"
Manuel Bonfim	"O Brasil"
Humberto de Campos	"Memórias"

Elysio de Carvalho	"Os Bastiões da Nacionalidade"
Felix Contreiras Rodrigues	"Novos Rumos Politicos e Sociais"
Angyone Costa	"Migrações da Cultura Indigena"
Benjamin Costallat	"Cock-Tail"
Afonso Celso	"O Visconde de Ouro Preto"
Euclides da Cunha	"Os Sertões," "A' Margem da História," "Contrastes e Confrontos"
Osorio Duque-Estrada	"Critica e Polêmica"
Alberto de Faria	"Mauá"
Raimundo de Farias Brito	"A Base Física do Espírito"
Jackson de Figueiredo	"Humilhados e Luminosos," "Pascal e a Inquietação Moderna"
Gregório da Fonseca	"Estética das Batalhas"
Laudelino Freire	"Graças e Galas da Linguagem"
Ramiz Galvão	"O Poeta Fagundes Varella e a sua Obra"
Agrippino Grieco	"Carcassas Gloriosas," "Evolução da Prosa Brasileira," "Evolução da Poesia Brasileira," "Estrangeiros"
Luiz Guimarães Filho	"Samurais e Mandarins"
Vicente Licinio Cardoso	"A Filosofia da Arte"
Medeiros e Albuquerque	"Quando eu Era Vivo"
Andrade Muricí	"Suave Convivio"
Oliveira Lima	"D. João VI," "Pan-Americanismo"
Oliveira Vianna	"Populações Meridionais do Brasil," "Raça e Assimilação"
Eduardo Prado	"A Ilusão Americana"
Alfredo Pujol	"Machado de Assís"
Eduardo Ramos	"Retalhos e Bisalhos"
Silva Ramos	"Pela Vida Fora"
Alberto Rangel	"Inferno Verde"
Garcia Redondo	"Carícias"

João Ribeiro	"Fabordão," "Folk-Lore," "Historia do Brasil"
Nina Rodrigues	"O Africano no Brasil"
Jorge Salis Goulart	"A Formação do Rio Grande do Sul"
João Pinto da Silva	"Vultos do Meu Caminho," "Fisionomia de Novos"
Paulo da Silveira	"Asas e Patas"
Felício Terra	"Contos e Crônicas"
Alberto Torres	"O Problema Nacional do Brasil"
Antonio Torres	"Pasquinadas Cariocas," "Verdades Indiscretas," "Prós e Contras"
Nestor Victor	"Crítica de Ontem"

PLAYS

Graça Aranha	"Malazarte"
Afonso Arinos	"O Contratador de Diamantes"
Paulo Gonçalves	"A Comédia do Coração"
Alvaro Moreyra	"Adão, Eva e Outros Membros da Família"
Claudio de Sousa	"Flores de Sombra"
Renato Vianna	"Berenice"

AFTER 1930

Representative Authors and Books

POETRY

Padua de Almeida	"O Instante Universal"
Murillo Araujo	"As Sete Cores do Ceu"
J. G. de Araujo Jorge	"Amo!"
Olmiro Azevedo	"Vinho Novo"
Raul Bopp	"Cobra Norato"
Wellington Brandão	"O Homem Inquieto"
Rossini Camargo Guarnieri	"Porto Inseguro"
Cleomenes de Campos	"Humildade"
Guilherme de Castro e Silva	"Poemas Novos"

Ovidio Chaves	"Cancioneiro"
Paulo Corrêa Lopes	"Caminhos," "Poemas de Mim Mesmo"
Athos Damasceno Ferreira	"Poemas da Minha Cidade"
Eliezer Demenezes	"Poemas da Hora Incerta"
Carlos Drummond de Andrade	"Poesias," "Sentimento do Mundo"
Sergio de Gouvêa	"Inquietação"
Francisco Karam	"A Hora Espessa"
Jorge de Lima	"A Túnica Inconsútil," "Tempo e Eternidade"
Edyla Mangabeira	"O que ficou de mim"
Cecilia Meirelles	"Viagem," "Vaga Música"
Murillo Mendes	"Tempo e Eternidade," "O Visionário"
Vinícius de Morais	"Forma e Exegese"
Emilio Moura	"Canto da Hora Amarga"
Reinaldo Moura	"L'Après-Midi d'un Faune"
Adàlgìsa Nery	"A Mulher Ausente"
Onestaldo Pennaforte	"Romeu e Julieta" (translation)
Mario Quintana	"A Rua dos Cataventos," "Canções"
Lila Rippoll	"Ceu Vazio"
Damaso Rocha	"Festa de Luz e de Cor"
Augusto Frederico Schmidt	"Estrela Solitária," "Mar Desconhecido," "O Canto da Noite"

FICTION

Moacir de Abreu	"Morro Verde"
João Alfonsus	"Totonio Pacheco," "Rola Moça," "Eis a Noite"
Oswaldo Alves	"Um Homem dentro do Mundo"
Gilberto Amado	"Os Interesses da Companhia," "Inocentes e Culpados"
Jorge Amado	"Cacau," "Suor," "Mar Morto," "Jubiabá," "Capitães da

	Areia," "Terras do sem Fim" "São Jorge de Ilheus"
José Americo de Almeida	"Coiteiros," "Boqueirão," "A Bagaceira"
Clovis Amorim	"Alambique"
Cordeiro de Andrade	"Tonio Borja"
Mario de Andrade	"Belazartes"
Oswald de Andrade	"Marco Zero"
Cyro dos Anjos	"O Amanuense Belmiro"
Graça Aranha	"A Viagem Maravilhosa"
Perminio Asfora	"Sapé"
Darci Azambuja	"A Prodigiosa Aventura," "Romance Antigo"
Tito Battini	"E agora, que fazer?"
Aurélio Buarque Holanda	"Dois Mundos"
Flávio de Campos	"Planalto"
Lucio Cardoso	"Maleita," "Salgueiro," "A luz no Sub-solo," "Mãos Vazias," "O Desconhecido"
Cecílio Carneiro	"A Fogueira"
Jader de Carvalho	"Safra"
Guilhermino Cesar	"Sul"
Antonio Constantino	"Casa Sôbre a Areia"
Felix Contreiras Rodrigues	"Farrapo"
João Cordeiro	"Corja"
Lia Corrêa Dutra	"Navio Sem Porto'
Dias da Costa	"Canção do Bêco"
Galeão Coutinho	"Memorias de Simão Caolho"
Gastão Cruls	"Vertigem," "História Puxa História"
Athos Damasceno Ferreira	"Moleque," "Menininha," "Burgo"
João Dornas	"Bagana Apagada"
Ligia Fagundes	"Praia Viva"
Octavio de Faria	"O Lodo das Ruas"
Guilherme de Figueiredo	"Trinta Anos Sem Paisagem"
Amando Fontes	"Os Corumbas," "A Rua do Sirirí"
Eduardo Frieiro	"O Cabo das Tormentas"
Rosário Fusco	"O Agressor"

Francisco Ignacio Peixoto	"Dona Flor"
Marcos Iolovitch	"Numa Clara Manhã de Abril"
Luiz Jardim	"Maria Perigosa"
Dalcidio Jurandir	"Chove nos Campos de Cachoeira"
Sra. Leandro Dupré	"O Romance de Tereza Bernard," "Eramos Seis"
Origines Lessa	"O Feijão e o Sonho"
Herman Lima	"Garimpos"
Jorge de Lima	"Calunga," "A Mulher Obscura"
José Lins do Rego	"Menino de Engenho," "Doidinho," "Banguê," "Usina," "Pedra Bonita," "Agua Mãe," "Pureza," "Fogo Morto"
Dionélio Machado	"Os Ratos," "O louco do Cati," "Desolação"
Raimundo Magalhaẽs	"Fuga"
Ciro Martins	"Enquanto as Aguas Correm," "Mensagem Errante," "Porteira Fechada"
Fran Martins	"Poço dos Paus," "Ponta de Rua"
Ivan Martins	"Fronteira Agreste"
Luiz Martins	"Lapa," "Fazenda"
Caio de Mello Franco	"Via Latina"
Rodrigo de Mello Franco Andrade	"Velórios"
Lucia Miguel Pereira	"Em Surdina," "Amanhecer"
Josué Montello	"Janelas Fechadas"
Vianna Moog	"Um Rio Imita o Reno"
Reinaldo Moura	"Noite de Chuva em Setembro," "Intervalo Passional"
Carolina Nabuco	"A Sucessora"
Adalgisa Nery	"Og"
Manoelito de Ornellas	"Tiarajú"
Miguel Ozorio de Almeida	"Almas Sem Abrigo"
Cornélio Pena	"Fronteiras"
Peregrino Junior	"Histórias do Amazonas," "Matupá"

Menotti del Picchia	"Salomé"
Ian de Almeida Prado	"Os 2 Sargentos"
Ranulfo Prata	"Navios Iluminados"
Raquel de Queiroz	"João Miguel," "Caminho de Pedras," "As Três Marias," "O Quinze"
Clovis Ramalhete	"Ciranda"
Graciliano Ramos	"San Bernardo," "Angustia," "Vidas Secas"
Marques Rebello	"Oscarina," "Três Caminhos," "Marafa," "A Estrela Sobe"
Nélio Reis	"Os Rios Correm para o Mar"
Othelo Rosa	"A Moça Loura"
Plinio Salgado	"O Cavaleiro de Itararé"
Affonso Schmidt	"Curiango"
Rivadavia Severo	"Visão do Pampa"
Dinah Silveira de Queiroz	"Floradas Na Serra"
Joel Silveira	"Onda Raivosa"
Miroel Silveira	"Bonecos de Engonço"
Tasso da Silveira	"Só Tu Voltaste"
De Sousa Junior	"Enquanto a Morte Não Vem," "Um Clarão Rasgou o Ceu"
Arnaldo Tabaía	"Badú"
Tetrá de Teffé	"Bati a' Porta da Vida"
Telmo Vergara	"Cadeiras na Calçada," "Histórias do Irmão Sol," "Estrada Perdida"
José Geraldo Vieira	"A Mulher que Fugiu de Sodoma," "Território Humano," "A Quadragésima Porta"
Alyrio M. Wanderley	"Bolsos Vazios"
Pedro Wayne	"Almas Penadas"

ESSAYS

Criticism, History, Biography, Sociology and Philosophy

Jaime Adour da Camara	"Oropa, França e Bahia"
Genolino Amado	"Um olhar sobre a Vida"

Jorge Amado	"A B C de Castro Alves"
Azevedo Amaral	"A Aventura Política do Brasil"
Clovis Amorim	"Eça de Queiroz"
Almir de Andrade	"A Verdade Contra Freud"
Tristão de Atahyde	"Estudos" (five series), "Ideia, Sexo e Tempo"
Magalhães Azeredo	"O Eterno e o Efêmero"
Fernando de Azevedo	"Ensaios," "No Tempo de Petronio"
Jayme de Barros	"Espelho de Livros"
Gustavo Barroso	"Historia Secreta do Brasil," "Terra de Sol"
Julio Bello	"Memórias dum Senhor de Engenho"
Lidia Besouchet	"O Visconde de Mauá"
Osorio Borba	"A Comédia Literária"
Rubem Braga	"O Conde e o Passarinho"
Sergio Buarque Hollanda	"Raizes do Brazil," "Cobra de Vidro"
Pedro Calmon	"História da Civilização Brasileira"
Luiz da Camara Cascudo	"Vaqueiros e Cantadores do Nordeste," "O Marques de Olinda e seu Tempo"
Edison Carneiro	"Castro Alves"
André Carrazoni	"Getulio Vargas"
Afonso de Carvalho	"Teu Filho não Voltará Mais"
Ronald de Carvalho	"Estudos Brasileiros" (four series), "Pequena Historia da Literatura Brasileira," "O Espelho de Ariel"
Josué de Castro	"Documentário do Nordeste"
Edgar Cavalheiro	"Fagundes Varella"
Lindolfo Collor	"Garibaldi e a Guerra dos Farrapos"
Dante Costa	"Paris"
Afranio Coutinho	"A Filosofia de Machado de Assiz"
Gastão Cruls	"A Amazonas que eu Ví"

Luiz Edmundo	"O Rio de Janeiro de Meu Tempo," "O Rio de Janeiro do Tempo dos Vice-Reis"
Alfredo Ellis Junior	"O Bandeirismo Paulista e o Recuo do Meridiano"
Octavio de Faria	"Machiavel e o Brasil"
Gondin da Fonseca	"Biografia do Jornalismo Brasileiro"
Gilberto Freyre	"Casa Grande e Senzala," "Sobrados e Mocambos," "Nordeste"
Eugenio Gomes	"D. H. Lawrence e Outros"
Castilhos Goycochêa	"O Gaucho na Vida Política Brasileira"
Donatello Grieco	"Napoleão e o Brasil"
Silvio Julio	"Cerebro e Coração de Bolivar"
Dante de Laytano	"Historia da Republica Rio Grandense"
Herman Lima	"Ceus e Terras da Europa"
Hermes Lima	"Tobias Barreto"
Alvaro Lins	"Jornal de Critica," "Correspondencia de Eça de Queiroz"
Edson Lins	"História e Crítica da Poesia Brasileira"
Monteiro Lobato	"América"
Washington Luiz	"A Capitania de São Paulo"
Roberto Lyra	"Tobias Barreto, homem-pêndulo"
Alcantara Machado	"Vida e Morte do Bandeirante"
Afonso Arinos de Melo Franco	"Conceito de Civilização Brasileira," "O Indio Brasileiro e a Revolução Francesa"
Oscar Mendes	"A Alma dos Livros"
Renato Mendonça	"Influencia do Africano no Português do Brasil"
Djacir Menezes	"Documentário do Nordeste"

Augusto Meyer	"Prosa dos Pagos," "Machado de Assiz"
Olivio Montenegro	"O Romance Brasileiro"
Vianna Moog	"O Ciclo do Ouro Negro," "Herois da Decadencia," "Eça de Queiroz e o Seculo XIX"
Carlos Dante de Moraes	"Viagem Interior," "Tristão de Atahyde e Outros Estudos"
Raimundo de Moraes	"Na Planície Amazónica"
Alvaro Moreyra	"Cocaina," "Tempo Perdido," "O Brasil Continua"
Arthur Motta	"Vultos e Livros"
Andrade Muricy	"A Nova Literatura Brasileira"
Berilo Neves	"A Costela de Adão"
Manoelito de Ornellas	"Vozes de Ariel," "Símbolos Bárbaros"
Silveira Peixoto	"Falam os Escritorés" (two series)
Peregrino Junior	"Doença e Constituição de Machado de Assiz"
Baptista Pereira	"Figuras do Imperio e Outros Ensaios"
Lucia Miguel Pereira	"Machado de Assís"
Aurélio Pinheiro	"A' Margem do Amazonas"
Henrique Pongetti	"Camara Lenta"
Eloy Pontes	"A Vida Inquieta de Raul Pompeia," "A Vida Dramática de Euclides da Cunha"
Caio Prado Junior	"Formação do Brasil Contemporaneo"
Paulo Prado	"Retrato do Brasil"
Arthur Ramos	"O Negro Brasileiro"
Cassiano Ricardo	"Marcha para o Oeste"
Rodrigo Octavio Filho	"Velhos Amigos"
Almir Rolmes Barbosa	"Escritores Norte-Americanos e Outros"
E. Roquette Pinto	"Rondonia," "Ensaios de Antropologia Brasileira"

Olyntho Sanmartin	"Terras de América"
Roberto Simonsen	"História Económica do Brasil"
Rivadavia Sousa	"Pé de Moleque"
Walter Spalding	"A' Luz da História"
Octavio Tarquinio de Sousa	"Bernardo Pereira de Vasconcellos"
Afonso de E. Taunay	"Visitantes do Brasil Colonial"
Limeira Tejo	"Brejos e Carrascais do Nordeste"
Moisés Vellinho	"Letras da Província"
Nelson Verneck Sodré	"História da Literatura Brasileira"

PLAYS

Joracy Camargo	"Deus lhe Pague," "Maria Cachucha," "O Burro," "O Sabio"
Ernani Fornari	"Nada," "Iaiá Boneca," "Sinha Moça Chorou"
Carlos de Lacerda	"O Rio"
Raymundo Magalhães	"Carlota Joaquina," "Um Judeu"
Maria Jacinta	"O Gosto da Vida," "Conflito"
Marques Rebello	"Rua Alegre, 12"
Oduvaldo Vianna	"Amor"
Renato Vianna	"Deus," "Sexo"

31564